Vegan Indian
Health, Wellness
Happiness & Longevity

GW01563321

Over 100 of My Indian Family's Secret Vegan Recipes Cookbook

Chutney, Naan, Chaats, Desserts, Pickles, Drinks & More!

By

Lakshmi Vemuri

Published by:

CSBA Publishing House

Cover & Interior designed

By

Sonia Singh

First Edition

Contents

Vegan Indian Cookbook

I have always been intrigued by vegetarianism and veganism. You know, I love animals, and I used to proudly say that to my friends and family. My mom always told us not to harm animals. Animals can't speak for themselves; they are speechless, so it's the humans' responsibility to be kind to them. We need to stand up for our fellow living beings. These were my mom's words every time she fed stray dogs.

But then we were non-vegetarians, and we consumed meat, ghee, curd, honey, and all of that on a regular basis. We had meat once every two weeks, but curd and ghee were part of every meal. My brother was not fond of meat, and he quit meat when he came across someone slaughtering an animal. From then on, he always preached to me about how bad it is to harm animals to satisfy one's taste buds.

However, my love for meat didn't let me go the path of any of the above-mentioned lifestyles. But India is a largely vegetarian country, with 38% of people being vegetarians. Truth be told, it's a lot easier to be vegan in India than anywhere else in the world. Honestly speaking, a lot of people here don't eat meat at all. And I had many vegetarian friends around me, which actually helped me turn vegetarian first and vegan next.

But, trust me, the non-vegetarian dishes with Indian spices are out-of-this-world delicious. No matter where you're from, you must've heard of Tandoori Chicken, Butter Chicken, and Mutton Dum Biryani, among others. Yep, they all are tasty Indian dishes with lots of ghee and meat.

I grew up eating those! Up until my teen years, I have been in a conflict between "I love animals" and "I need to stop eating animals." In this struggle came the meat cravings. The struggle was real. But one of my best friends saw me harping about this and going over and over again like a broken record.

Well, it was my 20th birthday, which is when my school friend gifted me a book, "Eating Animals" by Jonathan Safran Foer. Reading this book changed everything. It shook me so much; I cried all night on the first day of my 21st year on this little green planet of ours. Let me tell you a few things!

Every year, 20 million male chicks are being killed in the egg production industry. Hens in industrialized farms are given steroids, which makes them lay eggs 30 times more than their natural capacity.

In the dairy industry, infant calves are taken away from their mothers so that we humans could enjoy all the milk. Isn't it cruel?! The milk belongs to the calves.

Each and every year, humans are responsible for the

killing of billions of animals, including but not limited to pigs, cows, hens, goats, and many more.

Oh, the worst thing is, all these animals are killed in a reckless and cruel way. Oh yeah, there are strict slaughter regulations imposed by governments. However, several reports suggest that many slaughterhouses tend to ignore these so that they can save time and money.

After reading that book, I spent weeks researching and getting to know what humans are doing to the poor and innocent animals, just to satisfy our tongues and bellies.

Let me tell you a little more about myself. My name is Lakshmi Vemuri. I hail from the southern part of India. I'm a dental surgeon. For the last few years, I've been pursuing alternative medicines and diets. In this book, I'm going to introduce you to some of the best Indian vegan recipes that I've tried and tasted myself. But, before that, I'd like to talk about veganism, animals, and how my life changed after going the vegan way.

I had been a chubby girl all my childhood. Chubby, but not overweight. However, I had been diagnosed with

PCOS in my teens. Then, I had put on quite some weight.

My life has been such a struggle since that moment and for the years to follow. In my pursuit of weight loss, I had also discovered that the meat I was eating had contributed largely to my weight gain, along with my hormone imbalances.

Do you know, on average, vegans tend to be 20 pounds lighter when compared to meat-eaters? The saturated fat found in eggs, dairy products, and meat can cause inflammation in the body. So, I decided to cut it down. Six months later, I had lost 10 pounds.

Moreover, I don't know if it's a placebo or if it's the vegan diet's magic, but ever since I started this lifestyle, I have been feeling very good - I mean calm, composed, and overall happy. Maybe, it all comes down to not having the regret of killing animals for my food.

Anyhow, other than weight loss and some other mental health benefits, there are many benefits that a vegan diet has to offer. However, this is not a book about veganism and its benefits. I want to tell you about all the tasty recipes I had personally tried. Most of these recipes are designed, tweaked, and finalized by me.

I've spent a lot of my time developing these recipes. You see, no matter what diet I follow, I like my food to be tasty and healthy. So yeah, I've taken care of taste too.

Finally, you can't be a vegan overnight. My sincere advice for you all is to stress less and focus on one thing at a time and be consistent about it. You might fail a number of times as I did, but that's okay! I hope someday you will be a proud vegan.

By the way, all the ingredients used in these recipes can be found easily in Indian stores or online. Don't shy away from accepting help from your Indian friends.

Metric vs. Imperial Measurements

Being Indian, I was well aware of the metric system, which is milligrams, grams, and kilos, but as soon as I landed in the US, our baggage at the airport was weighed in pounds. On our way home, I found the speed limits in miles per hour. To end this confusion, as soon as I arrived home, I googled the difference between metric and imperial systems.

The US uses the imperial measurement system, which came from British rule. Even though the metric system had picked up steam, the American government decided to keep the British imperial system. However, most of the world, including India, uses the metric system. I will be using both systems in this book, depending on how I know the recipe.

Here is a brief table explaining the differences and how you could convert a measurement from one to the other:

Metric	US / 24 Imperial
1 milligram	0.0154 grain
1 gram	0.0353 oz
1 kilogram	2.2046 lb.
1 ounce (oz)	28.5 gram
1 pound (lb.)	0.4536 kg

1 stone	6.3503 kg
0 degree Celsius	32 degree Fahrenheit
24 degree Celsius	75 degree Fahrenheit

Defining Veganism

What does "vegan" mean, and how is that different from vegetarian and vegetable-based diets?

Veganism is a way of living that excludes the use of products that come from animals, such as food, clothing, cosmetics, or any product that's derived from animals. It is strictly against all sorts of animal victimization and atrocity. So, by now, you know vegans don't eat any products or byproducts derived from animal meat and its secretions like milk and honey. For the same reasons, the vegan diet is free from all kinds of animal products like meat, eggs, and of course, dairy.

Now, let's discover the fascinating story of how the concept of veganism took root. Although the term "veganism" was coined in 1944, this flesh-free concept has its roots traced back to ancient India and also from other Eastern Mediterranean societies. Disciples of Hinduism, Buddhism, and Jainism also believed in vegetarianism; they strongly believed that humans should not impose pain on animals.

One fine day, in November 1944, Donald Watson, a British woodworker, coined the new term "vegan" to separate himself from vegetarians who consumed animal products like dairy and eggs, but not meat. Veganism is an extreme form of vegetarianism.

Now every year, November 1st is celebrated as "World Vegan Day," a day for people who don't consume meat, milk, eggs, cheese, honey, ghee, mayonnaise, gelatin, whey, or anything that originates from our innocent animals. It's a day to celebrate vegans for going cruelty-free. They neither use clothing like leather, wool, nor the accessories originated from animals like pearls, ivory, or cosmetics made from exploiting animals. This animal-free holiday is to give a shout-out to all the vegans and celebrate their generosity.

Over time, many influential people who chose the path of nonviolence in the history of humanity adopted the vegan lifestyle. Do you remember studying the mathematical Pythagoras theorem in geometry? If yes, then you might know the legendary mathematician Pythagoras. Well, for centuries, he was the father of vegetarianism, but later, he adopted veganism. People who lived in Paris circa 1650 or people who lived in London around the 1830s were greatly influenced by Pythagoras vegetarianism. They would tout that they were going to be "Pythagorean" if they weren't eating animal flesh.

Until the 19th century, people used Pythagorean to describe a diet that was devoid of animal flesh. The meatless diet was named a Pythagorean diet. Until then, there was no such word called "vegetarian." The word vegetarian got coined in the nineteenth century. But, if you are wondering what made Pythagoras go vegan? Pythagoras strongly believed that all living things had a soul. He was certain enough of metempsychosis, which means the transmigration of the souls. In a lifetime, one could be born as a human, but in their next, they could end up being a pig and, in some cases, get slaughtered for bacon. So this thought belief led him to banish meat from his menu; slowly, over a period, his ideas evolved and led him to be vegan from vegetarian.

Great inventors like Thomas Alva Edison and Nikola Tesla and leaders like Mahatma Gandhi, Bill Clinton, sensations like Steve Jobs, and Oscar winners Brad Pitt and Joaquin Phoenix are followers of the vegan diet. Joaquin Phoenix, in his acceptance speech at the Oscars, rightly said, "no race, gender, or species had rights over another."

Why go vegan?

Various reasons range from moral concerns and religious beliefs to alarming environmental concerns. Furthermore, following this diet leads to an increased desire to improve health among people who follow it. In recent times, there is an increase in the number of people who want to adopt veganism through food, clothing, accessories, or cosmetics. Big thanks go out to animal rights activists and social media for creating awareness about animal agriculture and its subpar effects on the environment. They have vastly helped people switch to plant-based lifestyles in recent times.

Unlike vegetarians, where some just eat some kinds of meat or dairy, vegans stay away from all kinds of animals and their by-products, which include honey. Since vegans have a limited diet, they might end up being more nutritionally deficient than vegetarians. Vegans should keep a check on their vitamin B, vitamin D, calcium, iron, and many types of proteins. I made sure to curate protein-rich recipes in this book.

Please consider leaving a review online where you purchased this book. Online reviews will help my work reach a wider audience. Thank you in advance.

The Particulars of Indian Cuisine

Dals/lentils in Indian cuisine

If there's one dish that most Indians swear by, that would be dishes made from dal. Indians from every part love dal. Now, what is dal? Dal refers to pulses that are the dry and edible seed of a pod. There is a wide range of categories which include lentils, beans, and peas. So, in India, any split legume is called dal.

These pulses are available in the market in three different forms, like a whole, split with the skin, or split without the skin. Dal is made into curries, soups, desserts, stew, or sometimes eaten raw by soaking. Legumes are local and seasonal, like warm-season legumes and cool-season legumes, and might not be available in all countries. Whereas peas and lentils are usually readily available. They are in four different forms like whole and split, with skin or without skin. The skinless split ones cook easily.

Beans are sold fresh or cooked and preserved in cans. One great thing about India is they prefer cooking them fresh and homemade. Beans and lentils are cooked fresh for each meal. You will not find canned beans or preserved cooked ones in India. Cooking fresh beans takes a good amount of time. Since fresh one needs to be soaked for a few hours before cooking them, I have mentioned instructions about soaking and cooking time for them in this book. I have also mentioned the commonly available dals and also their substitutes in case you don't get them, except for a few like chana dal, urad dal, and toor dal, which I usually buy from the whole foods supermarket.

I have seen my non-Indian friends or someone interested in Indian cooking being amazed by the diversity and the range of fresh lentils, beans, and peas that go into Indian cooking. Indians are truly blessed to have grown up eating them all.

Why Legumes are so Important for Vegans

Legumes are best friends to every vegan. They are the powerhouse of proteins. They are capable of coexisting with nitrogen-fixing bacteria, which favors us by providing a digestible source of plant proteins.

For example, 100 grams of cooked chickpeas provide a whopping 18% of protein (recommended daily value), the daily fiber of 30%, 43% of folate, and is rich in manganese by 52 %. This crazy combo is proven to lower blood pressure, improve good fats, work on insulin sensitivity, and alter gut microbe imbalance for good.

According to science, consuming legumes can help your heart, appetite and help in regulating insulin as well as weight management. Legumes are an excellent source of the amino acid lysine and minerals like iron and zinc. By soaking, sprouting, cooking, or fermenting, we improve zinc absorption.

Busting Myths about Legumes

Can legumes cause inflammation?

Contrary to popular belief, legumes can reduce inflammation. This misconception doesn't seem to end at all. I often get asked about all the buzz around inflammation and humble legumes. Well, let me make it clear to you. Our modern science studies concluded that they have observed the greatest reduction in inflammation (C- reactive protein) when consuming a legume-rich diet.

Can legumes make you fat?

In fact, studies showed that there was a greater reduction in weight with a legume-rich diet. Furthermore, blood pressure and cholesterol levels fell when consuming legume-rich diets.

Are beans toxic?

If so, why are they not banned yet? Beans contain proteins called lectins which are found in many other foods. If beans are raw or undercooked, lectin can be harmful. So always cook beans thoroughly or buy canned beans.

Indian Legumes

Black-eyed Peas (raungi, chawli, lobhia)

These are a subspecies of cowpea and are available in most Indian stores. Although Chawla is commonly used in Indian cuisine, it is also common among South American cuisine. Widely consumed in India, the famous recipes of black-eyed peas in India are Kerala's olan or Punjabi lobi masala. I have mentioned both recipes in this book.

Chickpeas/Garbanzo Beans, aka Bengal gram/channa dal, Kala chana, or Kabuli channa

You probably would not meet an Indian person who doesn't love chana masala or chole bature, which are made from two variants of chickpeas. Chickpeas are in three varieties - brown garbanzo, white garbanzo, and split channa. They are called Bengal gram or channa dal (split and in yellow color), widely used to make sambar and channa dal in India. Kala channa are brown ones. Kabuli channa is a whole white pea, which is used to make hummus. Brown ones are substituted with white chickpeas.

Chickpeas/Garbanzo, split (chana dal)

These are split and skinned chickpeas. Chana dal is a staple in North Indian cuisine. You can find it by the name Bengal gram or chana dal in Indian stores. You can also substitute chana dal with split yellow peas.

Chickpeas/Garbanzo White Beans (Kabuli chana, chole)

These white chickpeas are the most used among all. You can find it in Indian stores by the name Kabuli chana. Which is used to make the mouth-watering chole bature. It is a Punjabi dish that is popular all across India. Chole stands for a spicy, tangy flavored chickpea curry, and

Bhatura is a soft and fluffy fried wheat bread.

Garbanzo brown (Kala channa)

These are brown whole peas, which are longer to cook but hold their shape well. They can be eaten along with salad when soaked or made into a curry.

Red Kidney Beans (rajma)

Since my childhood, I grew up hearing great things about the curry "Rajma." It was quite a popular dish among my north Indian friends. Red kidney beans are dark-red colored whole beans commonly made into curries, stews, or boiled with rice.

Split Black Gram(Urad dal)

Split black gram is soaked and ground into paste or flour and is most commonly used for healthy breakfasts in south Indian cuisine. Breakfasts like idli, dosa, vada, bonda, and papad. Whole black gram is named sabut urad. You can find both in any Indian store. Green mung beans can be substituted for these.

Indian Brown Lentils (sabut masoor dal)

Indian brown lentils can make a rich, spicy, creamy lentil-based stew. It is served for special occasions in Punjabi homes.

Yellow Split Green Gram (mung dal)

Split and skinned green mung beans can make many delicious recipes, but my absolute favorite is north Indian delicacy moong dal halwa. This dessert will surely steal your hearts, and I have an easy, tasty recipe for you.

Red Lentils (masoor dal)

Red lentils are split Indian brown lentils which are devoid of skin. It is a soft dal that doesn't need soaking and is easy to cook. Masoor dal has good acceptance by babies due to its texture that similar to milk. In India, it is usually fed from 8-9 months.

Whole Mung Beans (green gram)

Being South Indian, I grew up eating pessarattu, a staple

breakfast from Andhra, a southern state in India. Pessarattu is made by soaking whole green gram with the skin on. Then, the gram is made into a paste to make a crepe. Keeping the skin on the green grams makes it more nutritious and healthier than the skinless beans.

Split pigeon peas (toor dal)

I remember eating this dal every time I went to Punjabi Dhaba. The famous dal thadka is made of toor dal. Dal thadka is nothing but tempering the dal, which is one of the easiest dals to make. You can substitute toor dal with split yellow peas.

Yellow Split Peas

Yellow split peas are nothing but dried, split, and peeled seeds of the Pisum sativum plant. Through the splitting process, the outer skin is removed from the peas. Cooking time varies depending on how old the peas are. I would suggest you pressure cook the peas to save a lot of time. If cooking in a saucepan, the cooking time can vary from somewhere around 25 minutes to 2 hours.

Adzuki Beans (red chori)

These small red beans are grown across the Himalayas and East Asia. To reduce the anti-nutrient value, adzuki beans need to be soaked, sprouted, or fermented. By doing so, these beans are easily digested.

Cooking tips for Dals

1. First, sift through the pulses to remove any debris or pebbles. Then, rinse them thoroughly 2-3 times.

2. Pulses taste best when cooked at a simmer. Once you see them boil, turn down the heat to medium-low and cook at a simmer. You should always count the cooking time once it has come to a boil and not before that. For example, boil kidney beans for 30 minutes before putting them to simmer.

3. I remember my mom telling me that the older the pulses, the longer or double the time they take to cook. So there's no exact time. If you think your pulses aren't soft enough according to the indicated time, just go ahead and cook until your desired consistency. Make sure to add

more water.

4. If you are cooking in a slow cooker, use 3-4 times more water. If it's a pressure cooker or instant pot, 2 times more water is enough. You can add more water when it looks dry.

5. I can't stress enough on soaking pulses because it cuts down a lot of cooking time. Follow the chart below for soaking time.

6. As I already mentioned about how tasty they get when cooked slow, I highly recommend cooking in slow cookers, which also happens to be very convenient to cook them, just throw them in slow cookers in the morning and when you are back home from work, you have your food ready!

7. Kidney beans are known to be toxic until they are boiled for more than 30 minutes, and avoid slow cookers as they can make them more toxic. If you happen to use a slow cooker for kidney beans, boil them for 40- 50 minutes before using them, or simply use boiled canned beans.

Soaking Time for Indian Legumes, Beans, Lentils, and Peas

Whole green grams (Mung beans) - soak for 4 hours

Split green grams, with or without skin (split mung beans) - soak for 30 minutes

Split mung beans with skin - soak for 30 minutes

Split mung beans - soak for 30 minutes

Masoor dal (Red lentil) - soak for 40 minutes

Toor dal (Split pigeon peas) - soak overnight or at least 30 minutes

Yellow Split peas (Pea) - soak for 4 hours or at least 1 hour

Indian brown lentils (Sabhut masoor dal)

Garbanzo white (Kabuli channa) - soak for overnight or at

least 8 hours

Garbanzo brown (Kala channa) - soak for overnight or at least 8 hours

Garbanzo split (channa dal) - soak for overnight or at least 4 hours

Whole black gram (Urad dal, whole) - soak for 4 hours

Split black gram (Urad dal, split, with or without skin) - soak for 30 minutes

Red kidney beans(Rajma) - overnight or at least 8 hours

Adzuki beans (red chori) - soak overnight or at least 8 hours.

Tools for a Well-stocked Kitchen

Indian vegan cuisine is vast, varied, and, most importantly, very diverse. To cook these delicious Indian vegan dishes, you would need several tools in your kitchen to make your job easy.

These tools are pretty much easy to get since you buy most of them online no matter where you live. Moreover, I make sure that I list the tools that can be used for multiple dishes. Anyhow, here are the important tools you should have in your kitchen.

Kadai/Kadhai

The Indian version of a wok, a kadai is a deep pan made out of strong and heavy metal. It comes with two handles. It can be used to sauté, stir-fry, and also to cook curry. If you're cooking a dish that has a lot of gravy, Kadai is the way to go, or should I say, way to cook.

Usually, most of the kadais are made of alloys, mostly of brass, stainless steel, or aluminum. There are kadais available that come with lids as well.

Degchi

One of the most commonly used utensils in an Indian kitchen, degchi is a staple tool. It is a deep, round, and broad-rimmed pan, which is mostly used for cooking lentils, kheer, and several other dishes.

Made of copper or brass, degchi is also available in the stainless steel variety. Degchis are best suited when cooking large amounts of food, like biryanis. If you're planning to feed your friends and family, this tool could help you a lot.

Haman-Dasta/Mortar-Pestle

Not a cooking utensil, but this is a tool that helps you in crushing and pulverizing herbs and spices. When you're making seasonal pastes or spice mixtures, this tool is a must-have.

Usually, haman-dastas are made of wood or granite, but nowadays, you can also buy them that are made of ceramic or steel.

When you extract the authentic flavors of herbs and spices using this tool, the taste of your dish will be enhanced by a large margin.

Chakla-Belan

These are two different tools that go hand in hand, as they're used to make rotis, chapattis, and parathas.

Chakla is the rolling board that's flat and firm, made of wood. Belan is the rolling pin that's used to flatten the bread, whether it's roti or paratha.

Tava

A smooth concave pan like a skillet or griddle, Tava is a traditional Indian kitchen tool, which can be found in almost every kitchen over here. It's used to shallow frying Indian bread like parathas or rotis.

However, you can also use it to cook pancakes, omelets, and chapattis too. Over the last few years, tavas, which were traditionally made of iron, are now available in Teflon coated versions as well.

Pakkad/Chimta

The Indian version of tongs, pakkads are tiny tools that can be used to hold a steaming hot utensil while cooking. Usually, these are made of iron, but nowadays, you can also buy them which are made of stainless steel.

They come with a thick plastic insulation, for better grip. When you're dealing with a utensil that doesn't have handles, Pakkad comes in handy.

Masala Dabba

Indian food is rich in spices and herbs. And Indian vegan food is no different. To enjoy an authentic Indian vegan dish, you'd need to chime in some spices, which enhance the taste, and they're good for your health too.

Masala Dabba is a spice box, that can be found in almost every Indian kitchen. It is a large box with a lid, in which there will be several other small boxes or vessels. You can keep anywhere from 30-50 types of spices and herbs in there.

Idli Maker

Idlis are very popular in India, especially the southern part of the country. It's a famous breakfast dish that's rich in fiber and protein. To make it, you'd need an idli maker, which works similarly to a pressure cooker.

However, here you'll have a set of trays, in which there are shallow depressions. These are used to place the idli batter. The idli maker can also be used to cook similar batter-based dishes as well.

Staples of Indian Cuisine

Turmeric

This golden spice will never fail to make to the top of the list when it comes to Indian cooking. It was a staple for the past 4,000 years. Recently, they are available in capsules as a medicine for its immense health benefits.

Fenugreek Seeds

These bitter-tasting seeds are powdered and added to Indian pickles and curries. Fenugreek is quite uncommon in the western kitchen but it's been making its way to the west lately.

Cumin Seeds

These earthy flavored seeds are popular not only in India

but also in Latin and Central American cuisine. Cumin seeds are used for tempering curries which have a musky scent.

Mustard Seeds

Mustard seeds are widely used in south Indian and Bengali cooking. Always add mustard seeds first while tempering for any dish. Mustard seeds take a good amount of time to cook. Fry them until the seeds pop to add a mild peppery flavor to the dish. Mustard oil is a favorite among Bengalis. It is deeply valued and is a tradition for its pungent flavor.

Tamarind

The South Indian kitchen is incomplete without the tangy tamarind. It is used in south Indian dishes like sambar, pulusu, and rasam. My personal favorite is chintapandu pulihora. You will have all these recipes in this book. Chintapandu stands for tamarind. This dish is basically tamarind rice with a good amount of tempering. The tangy yet subtle sensation of this rice will make you want more. Pulihora is often offered is often offered to god.

Asafetida (Hing)

This is a dried gum-resin that's an extract of furula plants. It's ground to make a powder and is used commonly as a spice. It adds a savory flavor to the dish. The phytochemical ferulic acid is a good digestive aid and it's been used for asthma and bronchitis for ages.

Curry Leaves (kadi patha)

Leaves of the curry tree are called curry leaves. This versatile culinary herb is a staple in every Indian kitchen. It has a great fragrance which makes your dish smell amazing. I like to add some with tempering and once when the curry is cooked completely.

Jaggery (gur)

Did you know that white sugar, which is commonly consumed, undergoes a process with bone char? Let me explain it to you. Bone char is referred to as natural carbon. It is used by the sugar industry as a filter to decolorize the sugar. By this process, sugar gets its eye-pleasing bright white color. Jaggery is a raw, unrefined cane sugar, and it's totally cruelty-free with the extra benefit of vitamin B, calcium, copper, zinc, and phosphorus.

Tempeh

Tempeh is a traditional soy product of Javanese tradition. It is made by fermenting soyabeans. The fermentation process binds the soybeans to form a cake. It's a great substitute for meat in curries. You can find it in the refrigerated section.

Nondairy Milks

Vegans have various nondairy milks like almond milk, soy milk, hemp milk, full fat coconut milk, and cashew milk. I switch between coconut milk and almond milk for my daily Indian chai.

Nondairy Yogurt

For yogurt again, you can use soy milk, coconut milk, or almond milk yogurts. These are also available in supermarkets. Being Indian, we widely use coconut. I prefer coconut yogurt. You can try the brand "So Delicious" for coconut and almond milk yogurt. You can also try the recipe included in this book.

Nutritional Yeast

Nutritional yeast is an inactive yeast which is highly nutritious. It adds cheese-like flavor. It comes in powder or flake form; we will use both in upcoming recipes.

Grocery List

Spices

Asafoetida

Bay leaves

Black mustard seed

Black pepper

Black salt

Cardamom pods, green

Carom seeds

Cayenne powder

Kashmiri red chili powder

Cinnamon, sticks and ground

Cloves, whole and ground

Coriander seeds

Pepper

Saffron

Nutmeg

Spice Blends

Garam masala

Sambar powder

Rasam powder

Coriander powder

Cumin powder

Kasuri methi

Chana masala

Madras curry powder

Biryani masala

Chaat masala

Indian Dals

Dals - Legumes

Black-eyed peas (raungi, chawli, lobhia)

Chickpeas, garbanzo beans (kabuli chana, chole)

Lentils, brown; whole red lentils; Indian brown lentils (sabut masoor)

Lentils, petite yellow, split, skinned (green gram, mung dal)

Lentils, red/pink/orange, split (masoor dal)

Mung beans

Whole pigeon peas, split (tuvar, arhar, toor)

Red kidney beans

Split peas, yellow

Grains and Flours

Basmati rice, white or brown

Chickpea flour

Coconut flour

Coconut, dried, shredded

Cornstarch

All-purpose flour (Maida)

Whole-wheat flour

Nuts and Seeds

Raw Almonds

Raw Cashews

Raw Pistachios

Pumpkin seeds

White Sesame seeds

Peanuts

Dates

Fennel seeds

Sunflower seeds

Watermelon seeds

Tamarind pulp or fruit

Basil seeds

Chia seeds

Coconut, fresh shredded

Flaxseed

Golden raisins

Phool makhana (Fox nuts/ lotus seeds)

Nondairy Milks

Almond milk

Coconut milk

Soy milk

Cashew milk

Oils

Coconut oil

Sunflower oil

Sesame oil

Mustard oil

Peanut oil

Safflower oil

Other Ingredients

Rose water

Nutritional yeast

Tempeh

Tofu

Puffed rice

Flattened rice

Ragi powder

Indian tea

Jaggery powder

Dried rose petals

Soya chunks

Indian gooseberries

Kala namak (black salt)

Leafy greens

Spinach

Amaranth

Coriander leaves

Fenugreek leaves

Radish leaves

Mint leaves

Mustard leaves

Vegetables

Onions

Carrot

Radish

Garlic

Ginger

Chilies

Beetroot

Tamarind

Tomatoes

Potatoes

Ladies finger

Bottle gourd

Mushrooms

Corn

Green peas

Sweet potatoes

Cucumber

Indian Breakfast Recipes

Breakfast is nothing but breaking the long fast. Usually, Indian breakfasts pump lots of energy. Indian breakfast is usually made from rice flour, wheat flour, chickpea flour, or green gram flour. The dishes range from north Indian katchori, dholka, poha, and chilla to south Indian fluffy idlis or upma, paddu, and dosa and pessarattu crepes will definitely have your heart. The best thing is most Indian breakfasts call for fermentation and the use of fresh flour.

Chilla

Chillas are classic Indian pancakes. They are made from chickpea flour (besan flour) made into a runny batter and cooked as you would do for omelets. I call them besan omelets. Stuff them with roasted or fresh veggies or vegan feta. Add finely chopped vegetables such as zucchini or carrot. Chillas are a popular north Indian breakfast. Serve them with chutneys or ketchup.

Ingredients

1 cup chickpea flour (besan)

3/4 teaspoon salt

1 1/2 cups water

4 chopped curry leaves

1/4 teaspoon turmeric

1/2 teaspoon cumin seeds

1/2 teaspoon carom seeds

1/4 teaspoon cayenne

1/2 cup finely chopped red onion

1 hot green chilly, finely chopped

1/4 cup chopped cilantro

1/2 cup of groundnut oil

How to prepare:

1. In a mixing bowl, add in all the ingredients with just 1 tablespoon of oil. Now add 3/4 cup of water. And whisk to achieve a smooth consistency. Whisk in and add more water if needed. Make sure to achieve a lump-free batter. You will need less water for besan flour.

2. Now, let this batter sit for 5 minutes.

3. Heat the skillet on medium heat. Once it's hot, add half

tablespoon of oil onto the skillet.

4. Pour a spoonful of mixture and spread it like a pancake of 6-8 inches. Keep the flame on low to medium.

5. Now drizzle some drops of oil on the edges of the pancake.

6. Roast until golden brown on both sides.

7. And serve hot with your favourite chutney.

Dhokla

Although this dish hails from Gujarat, dhokla is famous all across India. Dhokla is made of a ground fermented batter of lentils. It is a spongy, soft, lightly sweet, and savoury dish which looks like a cake.

Ingredients

For the batter:

1 1/2 cup chickpea flour (besan)

1/4 teaspoon turmeric

3 tablespoon semolina

2 finely chopped chillies

1 tablespoon of groundnut oil

1/2 teaspoon fresh ginger paste

1 teaspoon ground jaggery

1/2 teaspoon salt

Pinch of asafoetida (hing)

1 cup of water

1 tablespoon lemon juice

1/2 teaspoon Eno fruit salt (Eno is 60% baking soda and

40% citric acid)

For tempering:

3 tsp of groundnut oil

I teaspoon mustard seeds

1 teaspoon sesame seeds

1/2 teaspoon cumin seeds

Pinch of hing

Some curry leaves

1/4 cup water

2 green chillies, slit

1 teaspoon jaggery powder

1/4 teaspoon salt

1 teaspoon lemon juice

For garnishing:

Some finely chopped coriander

2 tablespoons of freshly grated coconut

How to prepare:

1. In a large mixing bowl, add all the ingredients listed in the section for the batter, except the Eno fruit salt.

2. Now mix with that 1 cup of water or add more if required. Now mix them all until you achieve a smooth batter. Let is sit for 20 minutes. Now whisk it again and add 1/2 teaspoon Eno fruit salt or baking soda.

3. Transfer this batter into a greased pot and steam the batter for 20 minutes on a low flame.

4. Now, let's prepare the tempering. Take a small pan and add the oil and add mustard seeds, cumin seeds, sesame

seeds, chillies, salt, hing, jaggery powder, curry leaves, lemon juice, and lastly water and stir it well. Now cut the dhokla in squares and pour the tempering.

5. Now garnish with grated coconut and coriander leaves. Serve this with chutney.

Idli

I have eaten idli all my life, sometimes even thrice a week. Yes, I know that's a lot, but we are south Indians, and we love our idlis. Idlis are soft, savoury cakes made from lentil and rice batter. In India, idlis are a favourite among doctors. Idli is the only breakfast they want patients to eat when we are sick. It's one of the healthiest breakfasts one could think of. Use fresh urad dal as aged urad makes idlis dense.

Ingredients

Black gram (urad dal)

Idli rice/ Parboiled rice

Brown rice or white rice

Flattened rice/poha

1 teaspoon fenugreek seeds

How to prepare:

1. Soak all the ingredients separately for 5 hours.

2. Grind the urad dal into soft and fluffy consistency, and rice into coarse. Grinding can be done in a mixer grinder or tabletop stone wet grinder.

3. Mix both the batters and allow them to ferment overnight or for 8 hours.

4. Now add this batter into an idli mold and pressure cook, or simply steam them in a saucepan for 15 minutes. Make sure not to over steam idlis as they become dense. Enjoy them hot with coconut chutney or sambar.

Masala Dosa with Aloo Bhaji (potato curry)

This famous south Indian breakfast is one of the most popular breakfasts in hotels. The masala that's on a crispy fried dosa along with potato curry is just so delicious. Now let's see how you can make it.

Ingredients

For the batter:

1 cup urad dal

I cup flattened rice

1/2 teaspoon fenugreek seeds

3 cups brown or white rice

1 cup toor dal

1 cup chana dal

Water to soak

For potato curry

3 boiled and mashed potatoes

2 tablespoon oil

1 teaspoon urad dal

1 teaspoon mustard seed

1 dried red chilli

1/4 teaspoon turmeric

1 teaspoon chana dal

Few curry leaves

2 green chillies finely chopped

Pinch of hing

1 sliced onion

1 teaspoon salt

1 inch finely chopped ginger

2 tablespoon lemon juice

2 tablespoon finely chopped coriander

Batter preparation:

1. In a large bowl, take 3 cups of rice and ½ tsp fenugreek seeds, rinse them and soak for 4 hours.

2. Take another bowl and add a cup of urad dal,2 tablespoons of chana dal and 2 tablespoons of toor dal.

3. Rinse them and soak for 2 hours. Drain and water and grind them in the grinder. Add water to blend smoothly.

4. To the same grinder, add the soaked rice and poha, water, and blend to a coarse paste. Now mix both rice and

urad dal batter. Let it ferment for at least 8 hours. Now add 1 tablespoon salt to the fermented batter and mix well. It's ready.

Potato curry preparation:

1. In a kadai, heat 2 tablespoons of oil and add the mustard seeds, urad dal, chana dal, red chilli, curry leaves, and hing. Now add the chillies and ginger. Sauté well and add the onions until they are translucent.

2. Now add the turmeric and potatoes. Mash them well and mix them to combine. Turn off the heat. Now add coriander and lemon juice and mix well.

Masala dosa preparation:

1. Heat the Tawa in medium flame and add a spoonful of mixture, and spread it thin for crispy dosa. Spread the oil uniformly and place 2 tablespoons of aloo masala at the center.

2. Roast the dosa until crisp and golden brown. Now roll the dosa and serve it hot along with coconut chutney and

sambar.

Veg Paddu (paniyaram)

Since we now know how to make idlis and dosa, let's learn this dish which is made from the same idli batter. My mom makes this dish with leftover idli or dosa batter. Trust me, both taste amazing. While idli batter paddu are a little crispy, while dosa batter paddu will just melt in your mouth.

Ingredients

1/2 cup of idli or dosa batter

1/2 onion, finely chopped

5 tablespoon of grated carrot

5 tablespoon grated cabbage

3 tablespoons of rice bran oil

1/2 piece grated ginger

2 tablespoons of finely chopped coriander leaves

2 -3 tablespoon of torn curry leaves

Salt as per taste

1 finely chopped green chilli

How to prepare:

1. In a large bowl, add the batter and all the veggies and salt and give this mixture a good stir. Let the batter sit aside for good 20 minutes for fermentation.

2. Meanwhile, grease the compartments of a paddu maker with oil and heat on low flame. Once hot, add the batter and cover the lid and cook on a medium flame. Steam until they are fluffy.

3. Take out the paddus with the help of a spoon and serve hot with your favourite chutney.

Pessarattu

Pessarattu is a popular food from Andhra Pradesh. Pessarattu is made by soaking green grams and rice flour. Basically, it's a crispy green gram crepe. It's eaten along with upma and coconut chutney.

Ingredients

1 cup green gram

2 tablespoon chickpeas (chana dal)

Water to soak

1 tablespoon rice flour

Salt to taste

Oil to roast the dosa

Half finely chopped onion

1 finely chopped green chilli

1 tablespoon crushed jeera powder

1 inch finely chopped ginger

How to prepare:

1. In a bowl, soak the green grams and chickpeas for 8 hours. Drain the water and grind the grams and peas to make a smooth batter. Add water if needed.

2. Transfer this to a bowl and add the rice flour and salt. Rice flour gives crispiness; mix well and add water if needed until you achieve the consistency for dosa.

3. Heat the tawa on medium heat and add a spoonful of mixture and spread it thinly in a circular motion.

4. Also, smear the onions, ginger, jeera powder and chilli along with oil over the pessarattu. Press gently to stick the onions to dosa. Roast on low flame. Serve pessarattu with hot upma and ginger chutney (allam pacahadi).

Rava Upma

The traditional south Indian upma is cooked with dry roasted semolina or coarse rice flour. It's cooked by thickening the porridge, which just melts in your mouth. Plus, it just takes 20 minutes to cook. Upma can be loaded with veggies like carrots, beans, and peas. Here, the recipe is for plain upma.

Ingredients

1 cup semolina (bombay rava, sooji)

3 tablespoons sunflower oil

1 teaspoon mustard seeds

1/2 teaspoon chana dal

I dried red chilli

1/2 teaspoon urad dal

1 finely chopped onion

Few curry leaves

2 finely chopped green chillies

3 cups water

1 inch finely chopped ginger

1/2 teaspoon salt

3 tablespoon lemon juice

2 tablespoon coriander

How to prepare:

1. Dry roast the semolina on low flame for 5 minutes and set it aside.

2. Heat a large kadai and add 2 tablespoon oil, mustard seeds, dried red chilli, urad dal, jeera, and few curry

leaves. Sauté until the mustard seeds pop. Add the onion, green chilli and ginger and sauté them for 2 minutes.

3. Now pour in the water and boil vigorously. Add salt and turn the flame to low and add in the rava slowly; keep stirring to avoid lumps. Mix well and cover the lid and simmer for 5 minutes on low flame.

4. Lastly add the lemon juice and coriander leaves and mix well. Serve hot!

Aloo Poha

Poha is flattened rice which is from Maharashtrian cuisine. Among all kinds of pohas, aloo poha is my favourite. I mean, who doesn't like potatoes? We all love them, right? So try this recipe.

Ingredients

1 cup flattened rice (poha)

1 finely chopped potato

3 tablespoon rice bran oil

Salt to taste

1 teaspoon mustard seeds

Pinch of hing

1/2 teaspoon cumin seeds

1 finely chopped onion

Few curry leaves

1 finely chopped green chilly

1/2 teaspoon turmeric

1 tablespoon lemon juice

2 tablespoon finely chopped coriander leaves

2 tablespoon roasted peanuts

How to prepare:

1. Rinse and soak poha for 2 minutes. Drain the water. Add some salt and mix well and set aside.

2. Heat a large kadai and add the oil for tempering. Next, add mustard seeds, cumin seeds, curry leaves and hing. Now add in the sauté onions until translucent. Add chilli and ginger and sauté for 2 minutes.

3. Now add turmeric, potato, and salt to taste and sauté for a minute more. Cover the lid and cook for 5 minutes on low heat.

4. Now, add the poha and peanuts and mix them gently. Cover and simmer for 2 more minutes.

5. Turn off the heat and add coriander leaves and drizzle lemon juice. Serve hot along with Indian chai.

Besan Kachori

We lived in Chhattisgarh, a north Indian state, for a few

years, where my neighbours often shared some kachoris with us. Besan kachori is the simplest of all and is less time-consuming. So this was usually made for hurry-scurry Mondays. Which usually went into our lunch box and still tasted yummy. I provide you with a simpler recipe here.

Ingredients

1 cup of whole wheat flour

2 tablespoon of rice bran oil

Salt as per taste

1/2 cup besan (chickpea flour)

2 tablespoon rice bran oil

1/2 teaspoon red chilli powder

1 green chilli

1/2 teaspoon coriander powder

1/4 teaspoon fennel powder

1/2 teaspoon garam masala

2 teaspoon lemon juice

Pinch of hing

Salt of taste

How to prepare:

1. To prepare the dough, mix the flour with salt and oil, later sprinkle some water to form a dough. Let it sit for 20 minutes.

2. Meanwhile, prepare the stuffing. Heat the pan on low flame and add oil, green chillies, and hing. Now, add in red chilli powder, besan, garam masala, coriander powder, fennel powder, and salt and sauté on low heat.

3. Turn off the heat and add lemon juice. Knead the dough for a minute and divide into 8 balls. Make a bowl shape of dough and stuff 2 teaspoons of stuffing.

4. Now, gather the edges and seal it properly. Flatten it with your hands or a rolling pin.

5. Heat the oil. Once it's hot, add the kachoris. Cook on both sides until it's golden brown. Fry on a medium flame. Drain the excess oil on a paper towel.

Ragi Malt

Ragi malt is a healthy Indian breakfast drink that's light and healthy. This recipe is from Karnataka and is made with ragi flour. You can also make it with sprouted ragi flour and water. Topped with cashew nuts, almonds, and dried grated coconut. For toddlers, use almond powder as a topping.

Ingredients

1 cup ragi flour

2 cups water + 1/2 cup water

6 tablespoons of jaggery powder. Adjust as per your taste

1 cup of chopped mixed nuts

1 cup dried grated coconut

1/4 teaspoon cardamom powder

How to prepare:

1. Bring 2 cups of water to boil in a thick-bottomed saucepan. While it comes to a boil, let's prepare the ragi slurry.

2. To 1 cup of ragi flour, add 1/2 cup water to make a slurry without any lumps. Add this slurry to boiling water. Cook for 10 -1 2 minutes.

3. Lastly, add the jaggery and cardamom powder and mix well.

4. Serve it in a glass and add mixed nuts and coconut. Enjoy warm!

Indian Chai (Tea)

Indian breakfast is always eaten along with Indian chai. India loves chai. They start their day with a steaming cup of chai or drink along with breakfast. There are various kinds of teas in India. This is a basic chai that uses cardamom. You can replace it with freshly grated ginger. Enjoy this chai with breakfast or a snack.

Ingredients

3/4 cup of water

2 teaspoons of Indian loose tea

1.5 tablespoon jaggery

1.25 cup of oat milk or soy milk, almond milk

2 cardamom pods (crushed)

How to prepare:

1. Heat a small deep pan and add water, tea leaves, jaggery, and cardamom powder, or freshly grated ginger. Boil for 5 minutes.

2. Now, slowly add the almond milk and boil for 6 more minutes.

3. Strain it into your cup and enjoy!

Chutney Recipes

Coconut Chutney

This south Indian chutney is made by ground fresh coconut pulp, which has a creamy texture and buttery flavour and is widely eaten with all breakfasts.

Ingredients

Half a coconut, chopped or grated

1 teaspoon mustard seeds

Pinch of turmeric

1 tablespoon cumin seeds

1 garlic clove

2 tablespoon coconut oil

5-6 finely chopped curry leaves

2 split dry red chillies

Salt to taste

Water to grind

1 tablespoon split chickpeas

How to prepare:

1. In a small pan, add 1 tablespoon oil, and sauté the

chillies for 2 minutes. Now in a food processor add the coconut, salt, chillies, cumin, and garlic. Grind them into a fine paste, add some water if needed and keep it aside.

2. Let's add tempering. Take the same pan which we used earlier, add 1 tablespoon oil and once it's hot, add the mustard seeds, chana dal, red chillies, turmeric, and stir frequently till they turn brown.

3. Now add coconut paste, and mix well. Add salt if needed. And serve it with idli, dosa, paddu and enjoy!

Bombay Chutney

Bombay chutney got its name from the place Bombay in Maharastra, where it's hugely popular. It is consumed as a side dish along with poori, dosa, and idli.

Ingredients

I finely chopped tomato

2 tablespoon gram flour

3 tablespoon mustard oil

1/2teaspoon urad dal

1/2 teaspoon cumin seeds

2 cups of water

1 inch finely chopped ginger

1/2 teaspoon chana dal

Few curry leaves

1/2 sliced onion

1 slit chilli

1/2 teaspoon salt

Pinch of hing

1/2 teaspoon turmeric

1 teaspoon lemon juice

2 tablespoon finely chopped coriander

How to prepare:

1. Take a large bowl with 2 cups of water and 2 tablespoons besan. Make the lump-free batter. Set it aside.

2. Now, take a large Kadai, heat it, and add the oil and mustard seeds, red chilli, cumin, urad dal, chana dal, torn curry leaves, and hing. Now add the onions, ginger, and chilli. Sauté them until translucent. Add the tomato and cook until soft and mushy.

3. Turn the heat to low and add turmeric, salt. Lastly, add the besan batter and stir it well.

4. Now, cover the lid and cook for 10 minutes. You can adjust the water and make it a slurry or a thick consistency.

5. Turn off the heat and add the lemon juice. Garnish with coriander. Enjoy alongside any breakfast.

Alam Pachadi (ginger chutney)

This famous andra pickle is made with fresh ginger, jaggery, spices, and tamarind; it is my absolute favourite. It's sweet, tangy, and very fragrant. I love eating this with idli and dosa whereas, it is also consumed with hot rice for lunch. This recipe makes approximately one small bowl of alam pachadi.

Ingredients

1 Tender fresh Ginger of 3 inch

2 tablespoons of groundnut oil

1 tablespoon of chana dal

1 tablespoon of urad dal

4 red chillies

1/2 teaspoon cumin seeds

1 teaspoon coriander seeds

1 teaspoon fenugreek seeds

1 1-inch tamarind

1 1/2 tablespoon jaggery

Salt as desired

1/2 teaspoon mustard seeds

1 teaspoon groundnut oil

A few curry leaves

2 red chillies

How to prepare:

1. In a 1/4 cup of hot water, soak the tamarind. Peel the

ginger and chop it into small pieces.

2. Take a pan and heat 2 teaspoons of oil. Add the chana and urad dal, cumin, red chillies, fenugreek seeds, and coriander seeds and sauté them till lightly brown.

3. Now, add in the ginger and give it a good stir and turn off the heat. Make sure not to fry ginger for too long as it gives a bitter taste. Let the ginger sit in a hot pan with the rest of the ingredients and cool to room temperature.

4. Now transfer this to a mixer jar and blend along with jaggery, softened tamarind, and salt. Blend smooth. Add water if needed to make it a thin consistency.

5. Now add the tempering and serve this allam pachadi with pessarattu, dosa, or idli.

Pudina Chutney (mint chutney)

Mint chutney is popular in north Indian cuisine. It is made of mint leaves and goes well with kachori, samosa, Indian sandwiches, falafels, and kababs.

Ingredients

1 bunch of coriander

½ of cup mint leaves

2 tablespoon of roasted peanuts

1-inch ginger

1/2 teaspoon cumin seeds

3 garlic cloves

1/4 teaspoon jaggery

1/4 teaspoon salt

2 tbsp peanuts, roasted

½ tsp cumin seeds

2 tablespoon lemon juice

½ tsp chaat masala

1/4 cup of water

3 green chilli

How to prepare:

In a small blender, add in all the ingredients and blend into a smooth paste. Add water as required. Enjoy this with besan kachori for breakfast or with snacks.

Peanut Chutney

If you are someone who loves the flavour of peanuts, then you will love this chutney. This creamy chutney is made from roasted peanuts. I like to eat it along with idli and dosa. I also eat leftover chutney for lunch with hot rice.

Ingredients

1/2 cup fresh roasted peanuts

2-4 green chillies

1 tablespoon cumin seeds

1 garlic clove

Salt to taste

Water to blend

1 tablespoon groundnut oil

1 strand of tamarind fruit

I dried red chilli

A few curry leaves

1 tablespoon groundnut oil

1 tablespoon toor dal

1 tablespoon mustard seeds

1 tablespoon urad dal

1 tablespoon chopped garlic

How to prepare:

1. In a small pan, heat the oil and fry chillies. Add tamarind to soften it.

2. Now in a blender, add chillies, roasted peanuts, cumin, salt, and garlic and some water and blend to make a thin paste. Now add tempering in the same pan by heating oil add mustard seeds, urad dal, toor dal, dried chilli, garlic and sauté until golden brown. Lastly, add curry leaves. Add this tempering onto chutney.

3. Enjoy with steaming hot idli.

Indian Milkshakes

Karjoor Milkshake (date milkshake)

These golden brown fleshy dates from deserts are a powerhouse of nutrition and pump up a lot of energy and will leave you full for a longer time.

Ingredients

10 seedless dates

3 cups of chilled coconut milk

1/4 teaspoon cinnamon powder

4 chopped almonds

How to prepare:

In a blender, add the chilled coconut milk, dates, cinnamon powder and blend them into a smooth milkshake. Serve it in a glass and add chopped almonds on top. Enjoy!

Banana Rose Milk

I remember drinking this at Kamath (a popular food chain in India) for the first time. As a kid, I loved the way it looked. This pink, flowery milkshake is famous all across India. It originated in north India. This milkshake is made from rose essence; I also add natural roses from my garden.

Ingredients

500 ml of chilled coconut or almond milk

2 ripened banana

3 tablespoon of rose syrup

1 teaspoon rose water

3 tablespoon soaked sweet basil seeds

Fresh rose petals (optional)

Any nuts

Chopped almonds

Dried rose petals (optional) for garnish

How to prepare:

Add the chilled almond milk, fresh rose petals, banana, rose water, rose syrup, nuts, and blend to the milkshake. Serve it in a glass and add the basil seeds and stir well, and dried rose petals and almonds on top.

Thandai

This north Indian summer drink is usually made for Holi (festival of colours) and shiva festival. The masala is made from various seeds, and peppercorns blend into a thick paste and added to milk. It's indeed a treat to sip on!

Ingredients

35-40 blanched almonds

15 black peppercorns

4 teaspoons of poppy seeds

4 teaspoons of fennel seeds

2 tablespoons of watermelon seeds

10 cardamom pods

1 Liter of fresh coconut milk

1/2 cup jaggery

3 tablespoons of rose water

A few saffron strands

Sliced nuts to garnish (pistachios, almonds, and cashews)

Dried rose petals to garnish

How to prepare:

1. First, blanch the almonds. Soak the almonds overnight or soak them in hot water for 20 minutes. Peel the skin.

2. In a blender, add the blanched almonds, fennel seeds, peppercorns, poppy seeds, cardamom pods, and watermelon seeds. Blend them into a smooth thick paste. Add some milk if needed. Once this thandai masala is ready, you can store it in the refrigerator for 2-3 days.

3. Add 1 liter of milk to the pan and bring it to boil on medium heat. Once hot, take 4 tablespoons of milk and

add it into a small bowl. Now, crush saffron in between your fingers and add it to hot milk. Let it sit until it turns into a nice yellow color.

3. Once the milk starts to boil, turn the heat to low and add thandai masala. Mix well. Add the jaggery and mix well. Turn off the heat. Now add saffron milk to this mixture and stir. Let this sit for 30 minutes.

4. After 30 minutes, add the rose water and mix. Let it sit for 30 -60 minutes more. This is important to make sure that all the spice flavours are absorbed by milk before we strain it.

5. Now strain it with a mesh strainer. Press the thandai paste that's collected with the back of a spoon to extract more flavours from the paste. Let it cool in the refrigerator.

6. Pour this into glasses and add the sliced nuts and garnish with rose petals and saffron on top. Enjoy!

Kesar Badam Doodh

This saffron almond milk is a rich traditional milkshake that every Indian swears by. It is also quite popular in middle east countries. This goodness is loaded with nuts and saffron and, of course, almonds. Badam milk powder is readily available in Indian stores. Add some nuts and almonds to the powder.

Ingredients

3 cups of almond milk

1/2 cup of blanched almonds

1 teaspoon saffron

Sliced almonds

Chopped cashew nuts

Sliced pistachios

2 tablespoon jaggery

How to prepare:

1. Blanch almonds and peel the skin and grind them into a fine paste.

2. Soak the saffron in 2 tablespoons of milk for 30 minutes and store it in the fridge. Keep a few strands of saffron for garnish.

3. Boil 3 cups of milk till it is reduced to 2 cups. Now add the jaggery and almond paste as needed and mix well. Once the milk is frothy and creamy, add the soaked saffron and give it a quick boil.

4. Turn off the heat and add the pistachios, cashews, and almonds and mix well. Garnish with saffron strands. Serve hot or chilled.

Haldi Doodh

Haldi doodh is every Indian mom's favourite. It's a

bedtime drink for their kids. This milk helps us fall into slumber sleep. This milk has flavours of Indian spices. If you have trouble falling asleep, you should try this recipe as part of your bedtime routine.

Ingredients

2 cups of soy milk

4 cloves

1/2 teaspoon turmeric

3 cardamom pods

10 black peppercorns

Thin slices of almonds

4 tablespoons of jaggery

How to prepare:

Using a mortar and pestle, crush all the spices mentioned above into a coarse powder. In a saucepan, heat the soy milk and add turmeric and powdered spices and bring to a boil. Once the milk starts to boil, add jaggery and turn off the heat. Serve it in a glass and top with almonds. Serve hot.

Indian Curries

Chana Masala

This north Indian dish is also called chole masala. It is a staple and is eaten with poori, roti, or basmati rice. You can cook this dish with Kala channa (brown garbanzo).

Ingredients

800 grams of soaked chickpeas (soaked overnight or at

least 8 hours)

1 chopped onion

4 garlic cloves

1/2 inch peeled ginger root

2 tablespoon tahini

1 tablespoon turmeric powder

1 tablespoon garam masala

1 teaspoon salt

2 chopped tomatoes

1 tablespoon cumin powder

1/8 teaspoon cayenne

1/8 teaspoon fresh ground black pepper

Half juice of a lemon

Chopped coriander

How to prepare:

In a food processor, blend onion, garlic, ginger and make a paste. Cook this in a pan over medium heat for 5 minutes. Add the turmeric, salt. Add in the tomatoes, spices, and tahini, and cook covered for 5 minutes.

Now add in the chickpeas and stir, cook covered for 15 minutes. Add some water, garam masala, cumin, cayenne, pepper, and cook for 10 minutes. Turn off the heat, add coriander and lemon juice. Enjoy!

Beetroot Thoran

This Kerala-style beetroot thoran is a special curry made during the festival Vishu. The freshly grated beetroot and coconut curry is simple yet delicious. Enjoy this curry with hot steamed rice.

Ingredients

2 cups of grated beetroot

1 cup grated coconut

1 tablespoon cumin seeds

Few curry leaves

3 tablespoon groundnut oil

2 roughly chopped onion

1/2 teaspoon turmeric

Salt to taste

1 tablespoon chilli powder

1 tablespoon mustard seeds

1 tablespoon urad dal

1 chopped garlic clove

How to prepare:

In a pan, heat oil and add mustard seeds, urad dal, cumin seeds, turmeric, curry leaves, garlic. Sauté for a minute and add onions and salt. Lastly, add beetroot and cook covered on a low medium flame for 20 minutes or until beets turn soft. Add chilli powder and adjust salt. Finally, add grated beetroot and sprinkle some water and cook for 5 more minutes. Enjoy with rice!

Bendakaya Fry

This authentic Andra bendakaya fry is made with ladyfingers. This simple recipe just needs tempering, chopped ladyfingers, and some freshly grated coconut. All it takes is 20 minutes to cook this fry.

Ingredients

4 large cups of chopped (round 1/2 inch) ladyfingers cookies

1 cup fresh grated coconut

1 tablespoon urad dal

3tablespoon groundnut oil

1 teaspoon cumin seeds

1 tablespoon mustard seeds

1 teaspoon turmeric

Salt to taste

1 chopped garlic clove

Ping of hing

15 curry leaves

1 tablespoon toor dal

How to prepare:

Heat oil in a pan add the mustard seeds, urad seeds, cumin seeds, toor dal, turmeric, garlic, hing, curry leaves and sauté for a minute. Once lentils turn golden brown add the chopped round ladyfingers. And sauté them without lid in medium flame for 5 minutes. Now add some salt and cook covered for 10 minutes, stirring often. Lastly, add chilli powder and grated coconut and cook for 5 more minutes. Bendakaya fry is ready. Enjoy along with hot rice.

Rajma Masala

This Punjabi dish is made from red kidney beans. This creamy curry is called rajma. Rajma is made by soaking red kidney beans and are boiled with whole spices of India to make a thick gravy and is served with roti and jeera rice.

Ingredients

300 grams of kidney beans soaked overnight in 4 cups of water and pressure cooked in 3.5 cups of water and 1 tablespoon of salt for 5 whistles until soft and mushy.

2 tablespoon of coconut oil

1 teaspoon cumin seeds

1 cup of grated onion

1 chopped green chilli

1/2 teaspoon coriander powder

1 tablespoon fresh ginger garlic paste.

Tomato puree of 4 tomatoes

1 teaspoon of garam masala

1/2 teaspoon turmeric

1 tablespoon Kasuri methi

1.5 teaspoon red chilli powder

Salt per taste

1.5 cups of water

2 tablespoon chopped coriander

How to prepare:

To a hot pan, add the oil, cumin seeds, onion, chillies, and salt. Cook for 8 minutes, till it turns golden brown. Add the ginger-garlic paste and cook for a minute. Add the tomato puree and cook for 5 minutes. Add all the spices. Mix and cook for 10 minutes. Add the boiled beans along with its broth, and 1 cup water. Cook for 30 minutes in low heat. You can mash some beans for thick creamy gravy. After 30 minutes add Kasuri methi, coriander and mix well. Turn down the heat and serve with hot rice.

Tempeh Ginger Fry

This stir-fried tempeh with ginger and creamy coconut milk just takes about 20 minutes to make. The smokey flavour from roasted red peppers and the sweetness of onions and coconut milk make this a wholesome dish.

Ingredients

18 oz of tempeh chopped into 1/2 inch cubes

2 tablespoon sesame oil

1/2 teaspoon turmeric

2 roasted red peppers

1 thinly sliced onions

2 tablespoons of grated ginger

1 tablespoon garam masala

1/2 cup coconut milk

Salt to taste

10 curry leaves

1 tablespoon coriander powder

1/2 lemon juice

12 tablespoon sesame seeds

1 teaspoon cayenne pepper

2 tablespoon finely chopped coriander leaves

How to prepare:

In a pan, heat 1 tablespoon of the oil, stir fry tempeh until the cubes turn golden. Put them on a plate. Heat the rest of the oil and add onions, ginger. Add some salt, now stir fry until they turn translucent. Add turmeric, coriander, cayenne and garam masala, curry leaves, and mix well. Now add the roasted pepper and the tempeh, stir fry for a minute and add the coconut milk and mix well. Let the mixture get warm, now turn off the heat and add the lemon juice and garnish with coriander leaves and sesame seeds. Serve hot

Dal Makhani

This smokey flavoured black lentil curry from Punjabi cuisine was my restaurant favourite. I ate every time I went to a restaurant. It tastes best with Indian bread and naans

Ingredients

Soaked black lentil and kidney beans in 3 cups of water overnight and pressure cooked with 3.5 cups of water and 1 tablespoon of salt for 10 whistles in medium flame.

4 tablespoons of groundnut oil

1 grated onion

2 teaspoons of fresh ginger garlic paste

1/2 cup of tomato puree

1/4 teaspoon garam masala

1/2 teaspoon red chilli powder

Salt to taste

1.5 cups of water

Piece of charcoal

1/2 teaspoon jaggery

How to prepare:

In a hot pan, add onion and a pinch of salt and cook for 7 minutes; add the ginger-garlic paste and cook for 2 minutes. Now add tomato puree and cook for 2 minutes, now add the boiled dal, all the masalas, chilli powder, salt. Mix well and add 1/2 cup water cook uncovered for 45 minutes. Stir often. Now mash the dal and add jaggery and cook for 10 minutes. Now lastly, to add smokey flavour, in a steel bowl, add red hot charcoal and some oil on it and place the bowl on top of the trivet. You will see fumes coming from that bowl, close the lid and let it remain for 2 minutes, and you are done. Serve it with Indian bread and enjoy!

Malai Kofta

Malai kofta is originally from Mughal's cuisine. Malai refers to the creamy sauce, whereas kofta refers to fried balls. Malai kofta is fried balls doused in a creamy sauce.

Ingredients

4-6 boiled and mashed potatoes

1/2 cup corn starch

2 tablespoon chopped coriander

1 lb. form tofu

1 tablespoon lemon juice

1 cup of frozen green peas

1 cup finely chopped carrot

2 teaspoon garam masala

1 3/4 teaspoon salt

Groundnut oil for baking or frying

I roughly chopped onion

4 chopped garlic cloves

2 diced tomatoes

1/4 cup cashews

1 1/2 teaspoon garam masala

1 inch chopped ginger

1 teaspoon turmeric

1/2 teaspoon cayenne pepper

115 oz coconut milk

1 teaspoon salt

1 tablespoon Kasuri methi

Coriander for garnish

How to prepare:

1. Heat a large pot and add the oil, onion, cashews, turmeric, garlic, ginger, cayenne pepper, salt, cook for 2 minutes. Now add tomatoes, cover the lid and simmer for 15 minutes.

2. Transfer this to a blender and blend it to make a fine paste.

3. Pour this back into the pan along with coconut milk, but reserve 1/4 cup of it. Crush some Kasuri methi and add to the curry. Now, set it aside.

4. Let's prepare for kofta. In a bowl, mash the tofu until it's creamy to achieve the texture of ricotta. Now add mashed potatoes, coriander, cornstarch, lemon juice, salt, peas, and garam masala. Mix thoroughly and make small balls. If the balls are falling apart, add more cornstarch.

5. Now, fry those balls in a deep pan with oil. Until golden brown (5- 7 minutes) or bake them at 425 degrees F by brushing some oil on balls for 30 - 40 minutes. Flip them once in 15 minutes. You will have crispy koftas.

6. Add the sauce on top of it and add that reserved coconut milk, garnish with cilantro, and enjoy!

Navarathna Korma

This royal Mughal's curry means 9 gems (Nava Ratna), and korma means curry. The nine gems are fruits, veggies, and nuts. Hence named "nine gem curry." This dish is traced back to the 16th century and was famous among kings.

Ingredients

4 cups of chopped and boiled green beans, carrots, green bell pepper, and cauliflower or broccoli

2 cups of chopped and boiled potatoes

3 +1 tablespoons of groundnut oil

1/2 teaspoon cumin seeds

4 chopped garlic cloves

2 roughly chopped onions

2 inch roughly chopped ginger

1 large tomato

I chopped apple

1 teaspoon coriander powder

1 teaspoon salt

1/6 cup cashews

1 teaspoon Kashmiri chilli powder

1/4 teaspoon cardamom powder

1/2 teaspoon garam masala

1 1/2 cup water

1/2 teaspoon turmeric

1/4 cup golden raisins

1/2 cup full fat coconut milk

1 teaspoon Kasuri methi

How to prepare:

1. In a kadai, heat 2 tablespoons of oil, add cumin, onions, and stir fry. Now add ginger, garlic, spices, tomatoes, and stir fry for a minute. Now add in the cashews, stir fry for 10 minutes and turn off the heat. Let it cool.

2. Add this to a blender and blend along with 1 1/2 cup of water to make a puree.

3. Now, pour this back into the pot and cook on low heat

along with the boiled veggies.

4. Now add the coconut milk and Kasuri methi to it and stir.

5. In a small pan, add 1 tablespoon oil, cashews, raisins, and cook until brown. Now add this over the curry. Add apples on top. Mix it and serve.

Sarson Ka Saag

This dish originated in Punjab but is consumed all over north India. The goodness of this leaf-based saag made from greens like mustard leaves, spinach, fenugreek leaves, and radish is eaten along with maki ki roti. This combo is the most favourite among Indian people. Through this book, you will learn maki ki roti as well.

Ingredients

1/2 bunch of spinach leaves

1 bunch of mustard leaves

1 cup chopped fenugreek leaves

2 chopped onions

3 inches of white radish root

1 cup of chopped radish leaves

2 chopped tomatoes

2 chopped green chillies

2 inch chopped ginger

2 cloves of chopped garlic

1/2 teaspoon chilli powder

3 cups of water

Pinch of hing

2 tablespoon of maize flour

Salt as required

1 tablespoon of coconut oil

1 finely chopped onion

3 bowls of cooked saag

How to prepare:

1. Clean and chop the greens. In a deep pan, add all the ingredients under the list of saag, excluding maize flour. Cover the lid and pressure cook for 7 minutes. Pour the entire thing into a blender and add maize flour. Blend smooth.

2. Now, pour this puree into the pan and simmer for 25 minutes.

3. In a small pan, heat the oil, add onion and sauté till brown. Add the saag and simmer for a few minutes. Serve them with freshly chopped onions and roasted peanuts on top. Enjoy with maki ki roti.

Tofu Masala

This simple 15-minute tofu curry is a great choice for the party's when you have to make too many dishes. This tofu curry is made with a blend of Indian spices is just delicious. Enjoy this with naan, roti, or even steamed basmati rice.

Ingredients

1 large pack of extra firm tofu (1-inch cubes)

1 roughly chopped onion

1/2 inch fresh ginger

2 roughly chopped tomato

1/2 cup water

3 garlic cloves

4 tablespoon sesame oil

Chopped coriander leaves for garnish

1 teaspoon turmeric powder

1/2 teaspoon garam masala

1 teaspoon cumin powder

1 teaspoon coriander powder

1 teaspoon red chilli powder

Salt to taste

How to prepare:

In a blender, blend the onion, ginger, tomato, garlic to make a smooth paste. Add 2 tablespoon water if needed. In a pan, heat the sesame oil, onion, tomato paste, and fry for 2 minutes on medium heat. Add all the spice powders and sauté on low flame; now, add the water and cook for 2 minutes on low flame. Add the tofu to the curry and sauté it on medium heat for 3 minutes. Now curry starts bubbling, and it's ready. Turn off the heat and transfer it into a serving bowl. Garnish with coriander and serve hot with quinoa or any Indian breads.

Kerala Veggie Stew

This mixed vegetable stew from the coast of Kerala made with coconut milk, and Kerala spices was my go-to recipe for cold or rainy days. I enjoy this with my jeera rice.

Ingredients

2 chopped carrots

2 chopped potatoes

1 cup peas

15 curry leaves

1 teaspoon crushed black pepper

4 cloves

1 sliced onion

1 cup full fat coconut milk

80 grams of French beans

3 -4 freshly crushed garlic

I inch julienned ginger

3 green chillies

1 cinnamon stick

3 crushed cardamoms

2.5 cups of water

2-3 tablespoon groundnut oil

Salt to taste

How to prepare:

Heat the oil and add all the spices and sauté them for a minute, now add in chillies, garlic, onions, ginger, and curry leaves. Sauté them till brown. Add all the veggies and stir well. Now add the coconut milk and water, cook covered for 10 minutes or until tender. Lastly, add water, stir and simmer for a minute. Serve it with steamed rice.

Guthu Vankai (Egg plant curry)

Guthu vankai is traditional curry from Andra Pradesh and its popular in south India. It's rich with flavours of Indian spices, peanut and coconut paste. This is popular curry for weddings across south Indians.

Ingredients

6 brinjals (young eggplants)

1 chopped onion

4 tablespoon groundnut oil

1 tablespoon ginger garlic paste

10 curry leaves

1 tablespoon Tamarind paste or (soaked tamarind in hot water)

1 teaspoon mustard seeds

1 teaspoon cumin seeds

2 slit chillis

200 ml of water

4 tablespoons of peanuts

2 tablespoons sesame seeds

1 tablespoon coriander seeds

2 tablespoon fresh coconut

2 cloves

1 cinnamon stick

1/2 tablespoon cumin seeds

2 dried red chillis

How to prepare:

1. Roast and blend all the ingredients under the paste. Roast each of the separately. Add tamarind paste, salt, and some water and blend to make a fine paste.

2. Wash and slit the brinjal into 4 pieces but keeping the end and stalk of the brinjal intact. Let them soak in saltwater till you use them. Now let's stuff the brinjals with the paste. Heat the pan and add oil, cumin, chillies, onion, curry leaves, pinch of salt, and cook for 2 minutes.

3. Now add the stuffed brinjal. And fry for 2 minutes. Make sure to coat them with enough oil. Pour water and let it cook at a simmer for 30 minutes. Enjoy this with chapati.

Matki Curry

Matki is moth beans and matki sprouts cooked with Indian spice blends. It is a staple among the Maharashtrian and Karnataka cuisine. Often found, this curry is popular in Dhabas and eaten along with roti.

Ingredients

200 grams of sprouted moth beans

1 roughly chopped onion

1/2 teaspoon turmeric

4-5 roughly chopped garlic

2 roughly chopped tomatoes

1/2 inch roughly chopped ginger

15 curry leaves

1/2 teaspoon mustard seeds

1/2 turmeric powder

1/2 teaspoon cumin

1 teaspoon chilli powder

3 teaspoons garam masala

1 tablespoon chopped coriander leaves

2 tablespoon sunflower oil

Salt to taste

Half cup grated coconut

3 cups of water

How to prepare:

In a blender, add in the onions, ginger, tomatoes, garlic

and blend to make a smooth paste. In a pan add oil and mustard seeds, cumin, curry leaves and add the paste. Stir and sauté for 5 minutes. Now, add turmeric, chilli powder and garam masala. Stir and add the moth beans. Add water and salt. Cook covered on medium heat for 15 minutes. Add water if needed. Once moth beans are cooked add coriander leaves and coconut and turn off the heat. Serve hot.

Indian Bread

Naan

Although this dish is from Iran, it is the most popular bread in India which came from Persia. This is India's best-loved bread and also happens to be a foreigner's favourite; the most ordered dish at restaurants.

Ingredients

2 cups of all-purpose flour

1 teaspoon of instant yeast

3/4 cup of warm water

1 teaspoon organic granulated cane sugar

1 teaspoon salts

Olive oil to brush on naan

2tablespoons of coconut oil

3/4 teaspoon baking powder

1 teaspoon minced garlic for each naan (here, 8 nans= 8 teaspoons)

How to prepare:

1. In a bowl, add the sugar and yeast, pour warm water (hot water will kill the yeast). let it sit, and wait until it's frothy on top.

2. Now, add in the flour, baking powder, salt and oil. Stir it until it gets difficult. Now, on a clean lightly floured surface. Knead the dough for 3 minutes; by now it should be soft and smooth. If it's too sticky, add more flour.

3. Place the dough in a bowl and cover with a tea cloth; let it rise for 30 minutes. If in a hurry, you can skip this rising step; your naans will still turn out good!

4. Now flatten the dough and divide into 8 balls. Heat the pan over medium heat. Now roll each ball on a floured surface into 1/4inch thick oval shape. Now press minced garlic on the top side of naan to make it stick.

5. Cook it on the hot pan until the top side has large bubbles and the bottom is golden brown. Flip and cook for 2 more minutes. Serve it with dal makhani.

Poori

Poori is a deep-fried whole wheat bread made from whole wheat bread. It is eaten for breakfast or meal. You can eat it with aloo curry, chana masala or any curry. The famous combo chole bature is chole and poori. Kids love to eat it with jaggery or jam.

Ingredients

2 cups of wheat flour

1 tablespoon semolina

2 teaspoon oil

1/2 teaspoon salt

Water to knead

Oil to fry

How to prepare:

1. In a bowl, add 2 cups of wheat flour, 1/2 teaspoon salt, 1 tablespoon semolina and 2 teaspoon oil. Mix well; keep flour moist.

2. ow add water and knead it tight. Now make small balls.

Roll the balls using a rolling pin. Keep them a little thick. Now heat a pan with oil to fry the poori. Press pooris to puff them up. Splash the hot oil to puff fully. Flip it and fry till golden brown. Remove it and place it on paper towels. Now enjoy with chole masala.

Maki Ki Roti

Maki ki roti is a flatbread made of cornmeal. It is widely consumed in Jammu Kashmir, Himachal, and many north Indian states. Like most Indian flatbreads it is also baked on tava. Corn meal roti is eaten along with sarson ka saag. I have also mentioned sarson ka saag recipe in this book. Check that out.

Ingredients

3 cups of cornmeal

2 tablespoon oil

1 teaspoon salt

Some warm water

How to prepare:

1. Mix cornmeal, oil, salt in a bowl. Add warm water and knead into a soft dough. Due to lack of gluten, this dough behaves differently than the rest. Let it rest for 15 minutes. Heat the griddle.

2. Take two sheets of parchment paper. Divide the dough into 8 equal parts. Now take on the dough ball and add some drops of water and knead for a few more seconds. Place dough ball in between parchment papers and roll the dough into thin 4-5 inch roti.

3.Now, remove the parchment paper on top and flip the roti along with the bottom parchment paper onto the griddle. Now remove this parchment paper gently. Cook on both sides till brown spots appear. Now cook it on direct flame too.

Serve hot with sarson ka saag or melted jaggery.

Chapati

This whole wheat flatbread goes with any curry and is easy to cook. All it takes is 4 ingredients and 20 minutes to prepare chapati. Enjoy with any curry mentioned in this book. Kids also enjoy eating this with fruit jams.

Ingredients

1 cup whole wheat flour

2 tablespoons olive oil

3/4 cup of hot water

1 teaspoon salt

How to prepare:

1. In a mixing bowl, add the whole wheat flour, salt, and stir. Use your hand or wooden spatula and stir in the water and olive oil. Just enough to make it soft and elastic but not sticky.

2. Knead it on a lightly floured surface to make it smooth. Be prepared for this good arm workout. Divide dough into 8 parts. Roll each part into a ball.

3. Now, heat the skillet on medium heat and grease it lightly with oil. On the, roll out the balls on a lightly floured surface using a rolling pin to make this chapati. Once the pan starts to smoke, put chapati and cook on both sides. Flip every 30 seconds.

4. At this point, you can cook on direct flame for puffy chapati or skip this and cook on tava. Enjoy with any curry along with chopped onions and cucumber.

Gobi Paratha

Cauliflower is named gobi in Hindi, and paratha is a flatbread. So, it's cauliflower flatbread. Cauliflower, along with Indian spices, are stuffed into the dough and made into bread. These are crispy yet soft bread roasted on the skillet. Enjoy this with mango pickle or it tastes good even when eaten alone.

Ingredients

1 whole cauliflower (florets)

1-inch grated ginger

1 finely chopped onion

2 finely chopped green chillies

1 teaspoon cumin powder

2 sprigs of finely chopped coriander

1/2 teaspoon turmeric powder

Salt for taste

1/2 teaspoon flax seeds

Sunflower oil to brush on the paratha

Salt to taste

Some water

2 cups whole wheat flour

1 teaspoon sunflower oil

How to prepare:

1. In a food processor, add cauliflower florets to make it crumble. You can also grate it. Now, in a bowl, add the salt, flour, water, and 1 teaspoon sunflower oil. Knead it to make a smooth dough. Cover the dough with a muslin cloth and let it sit.

2. Let's making stuffing. In a bowl, add the cauliflower, onions, ginger, chillies, coriander leaves, cumin powder, flax seeds, and salt and mix them well. Adjust salt and spice. Divide the dough into equal balls. Keep some flour for dusting. On a lightly floured surface, roll out the dough into a circle of 5-inch diameter. Spoon in a good amount of filling and place it on a half-circle of the dough. And press the other half to cover it and seal it. Dust this lightly on flour and roll gently. With very little pressure, roll the paratha in all directions. Make sure the filling doesn't ooze out.

3. Now, let's cook the paratha. Heat a roti tawa or skillet. Preheat it and place the paratha on it. Let it cook on low-medium flame for 2 minutes and flip or until brown its spots; brush some oil on both sides as you flip. It should be golden brown on both sides. Serve it with Indian pickles or curd for breakfast or as a meal.

Spinach Tofu Phulka

Phulkas are a staple in Gujarati cuisine. Spinach, whole wheat, and soft tofu are combined into the dough which makes these phulkas super nutritious. Try out these healthy green phulkas from the recipe below.

Ingredients:

3 cups of cleaned spinach

2 cups whole wheat flour

5 oz soft tofu

1/2 teaspoon cumin powder

1/2 teaspoon salt

2 tablespoon peanut oil

How to prepare:

1. Boil the clean spinach in a pot of water for 3-4 minutes. Strain it and put spinach into ice water for 3-4 minutes. Once it has cooled down, strain it. You can squeeze out the water by pressing it. Add spinach and tofu (without water) into a blender and blend to a smooth paste. Don't add any water for blending. This paste makes about 1 cup of paste.

2. Now, in a bowl, combine the tofu paste, whole wheat, cumin powder, salt and mix well. Knead the dough, add water if needed to bring the dough together. The consistency should be firm. Let the dough sit covered for 10 minutes. Add 2 tablespoons of oil to the dough and knead it again to make it smooth.

3. Make equal parts of balls from the dough. On a floured surface start with rolling the rotis with a rolling pin. Roll then thin and big. Use more dry flour as you roll.

4. Heat the skillet; once hot, put the roti and cook for 30 seconds and flip until brown spots appear on both sides. Enjoy with dal makhani.

Jolada Roti (jowar roti)

Jowar roti is a staple food which is eaten daily in households of Karnataka. These rotis are high in fiber, which is why people switch for jowar roti from rice when being weight cautious. It is eaten mostly with soaked legume curries along with raw radish leaves, fenugreek leaves, onion, and radish slices on the side. Ragi is a substitute for jowar. Replace the jowar with ragi and follow the process as it is to make ragi roti.

Ingredients

1 cup jowar flour

1 1/2 cup hot water

Salt to taste

1 cup jowar flour for dusting

How to prepare:

1. Bring the water to boil and once it starts to boil, add salt and sprinkle some jowar flour. Turn off the heat and add the rest of the flour to the boiling water. Mix it with any large spoon (water will be very hot). Let it cool. Knead with your hand when it is still warm. It should be soft if it's hard to sprinkle some water.

2. Make the dough into equal balls. On a lightly floured surface, roll the dough and flatten it by pressing uniformly. Roll it with a rolling pin as we do for chapatis. Authentic roti is pat thin with hands. which needs a lot of practice. Cook it on a hot skillet. Dip a thin cloth in water and wipe the roti to make it moist. Let the water evaporate to flip it to the other side.

3. Press gently with a dry cloth to puff up roti. Enjoy this with guthu vankai or garlic chutney.

Indian Stews

Tamil Nadu Sambar

This south Indian vegetable and lentil stew is delicious.
You can enjoy this with dosa, idli, steamed rice, and vada.
The tangy sweet flavours of sambar will have your heart.

Ingredients

1 tablespoon of tamarind pulp or tamarind soaked in hot

water for 20 minutes.

100 grams pigeon pea lentils

1.75 cups water

2 cups of chopped vegetables like carrots, French beans, peas, small brinjals, potatoes.

1 cup of scraped and chopped drumsticks into 4 inches.

1 thickly sliced onions

1 chopped tomato

1/2 teaspoon turmeric

2 cups of water

1/4 teaspoon chilli powder

Salt to taste

1.5 tablespoon sambar powder

2 tablespoon chopped coriander

1 tablespoon sesame oil

1 tablespoon mustard seeds

1 tablespoon fenugreek seeds

15 curry leaves

Pinch of hing

2 dried slit red chillies

How to prepare:

1. Rinse the pigeon peas and add them to the pressure cooker along with 1.75 cups water and let it cook for 7 whistles or 12 minutes on medium flame. Don't open it until its pressure settles down. The dal should be mushy.

2. In a pan, add all the vegetables mentioned above except coriander. Also, add turmeric, chilli powder, and 2 cups of water and cook till they are soft. Once cooked, add the tamarind pulp and sambar powder and mix well.

3. Now, add in the dal and simmer till the frothy layer appears. Turn down the heat and cover the lid.

4. Lastly, add tempering by heating sesame oil, add mustard seeds, dry chilies, fenugreek seeds, curry leaves, and hing. Add this tempering into the sambar. Enjoy this along with breakfast or for lunch with rice.

South Indian Rasam

A south Indian meal is incomplete without rasam. Every south Indian house has its recipe figured out. This thin broth is a staple among south Indians and is eaten with steamed rice along with potato fry or pappads.

Ingredients

1 tablespoon cumin seeds

4-5 peppercorns

3 garlic cloves

1 sprig fresh coriander stem

2 tablespoon groundnut oil

1 teaspoon mustard seeds

2 dried red chilli

15 curry leaves

1 chopped tomato

Pinch of hing

1 slit chilli

Salt as per taste

3 cups of water

1 cup tamarind pulp or soak 1 strand of tamarind in hot water

1 sprig finely chopped coriander

How to prepare:

1. In a small blender, mix the cumin, pepper, garlic cloves, coriander stem into a coarse paste. Do not add water.

2. Take a large pan, heat the oil, and add mustard, dried chilli, hing, and curry leaves. Now add the blended paste and sauté for a minute. Now add the tomato, salt, chilli, turmeric, and sauté for 1 minute. Now add the tamarind pulp and 3 cups of water and stir. Cover for 8 minutes.

3. Lastly, add 2 tablespoon coriander and enjoy this rasam with steamed rice.

Mulangi Saaru

This recipe from Karnataka is my favourite sambar. Its made of fresh radish, lentils, and fresh grated coconut.

This is eaten with breakfasts like idli, dosa, vada, or rice. I love the steamed rice and mulange saaru combo.

Ingredients

1.5 cup radish (mullangi)

1 thickly sliced onion

1/4 teaspoon turmeric

15 curry leaves

1/2 cup tamarind pulp or soak tamarind in hot water for 20 minutes

1 teaspoon jaggery

1 cut water

Salt as per taste

3/4 cup cooked toor dal

2 teaspoon sesame oil

3/4 teaspoon cumin seeds

2 teaspoon coriander seeds

1 teaspoon urad dal

4 dried red chilli

1/2 cup water

1/2 cup grated coconut

15 curry leaves

1 teaspoon mustard seeds

2 teaspoon sesame oil

How to prepare:

1. Add the toor dal and add 1 cup water and cook for 6

whistles.

2. In a kadai, add 1 cup water, radish, turmeric, onion, and few curry leaves. Mix them and cover the lid and boil for 5 minutes. We want half-cooked radish.

3. Now add tamarind pulp, jaggery, and salt. Mix well and boil for 5 more minutes. Now, add toor dal and the masala paste. Adjust the consistency, boil for 5 minutes. By now, the raw smell of coconut should wear off.

4. Add tempering with oil, mustard seeds, and curry leaves; pour this on sambar. Enjoy with steamed rice.

Pulihora

Pulihora is a traditional Andra recipe made during special occasions. Every festival calls for pulihora. It is offered to god. Puli stands for "sour taste," that's how it got its name since it's made of tamarind pulp mixed with rice. Adding a good amount of tempering adds a pleasant taste to pulihora.

Ingredients

4 cups cooked rice

1/2 cup tamarind pulp

2 dried red chilis

20 curry leaves

1 tablespoon urad dal

1 tablespoon of chana dal

1 teaspoon jaggery

1 tablespoon of mustard seeds

1/2 cup peanuts

1/2 teaspoon hing

4 slit green chillis

11/2 teaspoon Salt

1 tablespoon turmeric

2 tablespoon groundnut oil

2 inch finely chopped ginger

How to prepare:

1. First, mix the tamarind pulp, salt, turmeric, and hot rice and set it aside.

2. Heat the pan along with oil on medium heat. Once hot, add the mustard seeds, peanuts, urad dal, chana dal, ginger, and keep stirring frequently. Once they are slightly brown, add the dried red chilli, green chilli, curry leaves and pinch of hing and turn off the heat.

3. Now, add this tempering on to the rice and mix well. By now, rice would have absorbed the salt and tangy flavour from tamarind; adjust salt if needed. Enjoy.

Coconut Milk Pulao

Coconut rice is popular among Sri Lankan and Burmese cuisine. Sri Lankan and Indian cuisines have a lot in common. After all, Sri Lanka was once a part of India. Coconut rice is a staple among them and called Kiribati, which is eaten along with lunu miris. Here, this coconut rice slightly differs from it and has Indian spices and flavours.

Ingredients

2 tablespoon groundnut oil

1 teaspoon black cumin seeds

1/2 teaspoon fennel

1 cup basmati rice (soaked for 20 minutes)

1 cup mint leaves

1 cinnamon stick

3 cardamom pods

2 bay leaves

1 1/2 tablespoon ginger garlic paste

4 peppercorns

4 cloves

3 star anise

4 slit green chillies

2 cup of coconut milk

1 sliced onion

1 finely chopped carrot

2 tablespoon coriander

2 tablespoon peas

5 chopped beans.

Salt to taste

How to prepare:

In a cooker, heat the oil and add the spices, add onion, chilli, and ginger garlic paste and sauté till the aroma lasts, now add in the beans, carrots and peas, mint, and sauté for another minute. Now, add the 2 cup coconut milk and mix well. Now add the salt and basmati rice. Let it cook on the cooker, adjust salt while the rice is boiling. Now, add the 2 tablespoon coriander. Enjoy with raitha or mirchi ka salan.

Kitchidi

Although kitchidi is underrated, kitchidi has a rich history and has been hailed for its wholesome goodness in Ayurveda. This dish is devoid of all those strong spices and makes it to the top list of comfort foods.

Ingredients

1/2 cup basmati rice (soaked for 30 minutes)

1/4 teaspoon turmeric

1/2 teaspoon salt

1/2 cup moong dal (soaked for 30 minutes)

3 1/4 cup water

1/2 teaspoon salt

1 teaspoon cumin

1 chopped onion

1 chopped tomato

1/2 inch finely chopped ginger

1 chopped green chili

Pinch of hing

How to prepare:

In a pan, heat the oil and add cumin seeds, onion, and sauté until translucent. Now, add chillies, tomatoes, and ginger. Stir and add turmeric, hing, and stir. Now drain and add the rice and moong dal, water, salt, and cook covered for 7 whistles on high flame. Add water to adjust the thickness. Serve hot!

Palak Pulao

Palak pulao is spinach rice with Indian spices and some veggies. Its healthy, delicious, and colourful rice was often my lunch box staple dish. You can add any manner of your favourite veggies.

Ingredients

1 cup cooked basmati rice

1 teaspoon any oil

1 cup finely chopped spinach

Salt to taste

1 cup mint leaves

1/4 cup of fresh or frozen peas

1 thinly sliced onion

2 green chillis

How to prepare:

In a pan, add the oil, chopped onions, green chillies, and sauté till translucent. Now, add spinach and sauté for a minute. Once the spinach is cooked, add peas, salt and fry them. Now add in the cooked rice and mix well and cook for a minute. Mix well and serve the hot palak pulao along with raitha.

Soya Chunks Biryani

Biryani is a rice dish that originated among Muslims in India. Soya chunks are marinated to add flavours and are cooked with rice; soya chunks are one of the highest sources of proteins vegans opt for. Enjoy the soya chunk biryani with raitha.

Ingredients

1/2 cup boiled soya chunks

3 tablespoons of any oil

1/2 cup basmati rice (soaked for 20 minutes)

2 tablespoon non-dairy yoghurt

1 cup mint leaves

1 bunch coriander leaves

4 cloves

2 cups of water

1 cinnamon stick

3 cardamom pods

2 star anise

1 tablespoon biryani masala or gram masala

1 roughly chopped onion

4 green chillies

1 tablespoon ginger garlic paste

Salt as per taste

How to prepare:

1. Squeeze the excess water from soya and take them to a bowl. In a blender, blend chillies, mint, coriander leaves into a paste. Add this paste to soya chunks, along with ginger garlic paste and yoghurt and marinate and set it aside for 15- 30 minutes.

2. Meanwhile, in a pan, heat the oil, add all the spices,

onion, and sauté for 2 minutes. Now add the marinated soya chunks and fry for 2 minutes. Stir frequently.

3. Add the biryani masala and water, adjust salt and bring it to boil. Cook on low flame for 15 minutes. Serve with raitha.

Jeera Rice

This is probably the easiest rice recipe you will ever cook. This simple flavoured rice is made from cumin seeds. My mom always cooked this with leftover rice. It was my lunch box recipe for all those lazy days.

Ingredients

1/2 cup cooked basmati rice

1/2 teaspoon salt

1 teaspoon sesame oil

1 tablespoon cumin seeds

2 tablespoon coriander

How to prepare:

In a pan, heat the oil and add cumin seeds. And once they splutter, add basmati rice and salt and mix well. Lastly, add in the coriander leaves and enjoy with mirchi ka salan or dal.

Raitha

Raitha is a yoghurt and veggie mix eaten along with biryani. Here we are making vegetable raitha. This dish can be made in less than 10 minutes.

Ingredients

1/2 cup finely chopped cucumber

1/2 cup grated carrot

2 cups non-dairy yoghurt

1 finely chopped tomato

1 thinly sliced onion

1 tablespoon chopped coriander

1 teaspoon cumin powder

1 teaspoon salt

How to prepare:

In a bowl, throw in all the ingredients. Mix them well.
Enjoy with biryani or pulao.

Mirchi Ka Salan

This dish from Hyderabad is always an unsung hero and
always comes with biryani. This is made of chilis and
peanuts, which is extremely tasty. I like to eat it along
with coconut rice or jeera rice.

Ingredients

10-12 fat chillies (non-spicy variants)

1/2 teaspoon mustard

2 cups of water

1 tablespoon tamarind soaked in 1/3 cup of hot water

1/2 teaspoon kalonji

15 curry leaves

1/2 teaspoon cumin seeds

Salt

3 tablespoon coconut oil

1/4 cup roasted peanuts

1/4 cup grated coconut

1 sliced onion

3 garlic cloves

1.5 tablespoon roasted sesame seeds

1/2 inch ginger

1/2 teaspoon turmeric powder

1/2 teaspoon red chili powder

1/2 cup water

1/2 teaspoon garam masala

How to prepare:

1. In a pan, dry roast the onion, coconut, ground nuts, and sesame seeds for 2 minutes. Add these to a blender along with ginger, garlic, some water and blend to make a thick paste.

2. Now, slit the chilies vertically and fry them on a pan with some oil until brown. In the same pan, add some oil,

mustard seeds, kalonji and cumin seeds, curry leaves, and ground masala paste and fry for 5 minutes. Until oil oozes out on top and sides.

3. Add the tamarind pulp and 2 cups of water. Stir and cook on low heat for 5 minutes. Add the chillies, salt, and simmer for 6 minutes. Garnish with coriander leaves. Serve hot with any flavoured rice or chapathi

Indian Appetizers

Hariyali Kebabs

These versatile kebabs are made of green leafy veggies like spinach, amaranthus, coriander leaves. The best thing about these kebabs are that kids love these super nutritious green kebabs.

Ingredients

1 cup soaked chana dal for 5 hours

1/2 cup spinach

1/2 cup coriander leaves

2 finely chopped green chilies

1/2 cup amaranthus leaves

Salt

1/2 teaspoon amchur

1/2 teaspoon Coriander powder

1/2 teaspoon Nutmeg powder

1 cup chickpea flour

1/2 cup oil

How to prepare:

1. In a blender, blend the chana dal, amaranthus, coriander leaves, salt, green chillies. Transfer this paste to a bowl and add chickpea flour, amchur, coriander powder, nutmeg powder and mix well.

2. Make small dumplings of this mixture.

3. Now brush them with oil and shallow fry the kebabs on pan until golden brown. Serve hot with chutneys.

Veg Lollipop

Veg lollipops are crispy fried balls made of vegetable stuffing; these are crunchy from the outside but soft on the inside. These lollipops just melt in your mouth.

Ingredients

2 tablespoon grated carrot

2 boiled potatoes

2 tablespoon finely chopped capsicum

1/2 finely chopped onion

3 tablespoon fresh peas

3 tablespoon fresh corn

1/2 teaspoon red chilli powder

1/4 teaspoon garam masala

Salt to taste

2 tablespoon chopped coriander

2 cups bread crumbs

1/2 teaspoon amchur

1/2 teaspoon chat masala

1/2 teaspoon ginger garlic paste

2 tablespoon of all-purpose flour

2 tablespoon corn flour

1/2 cup water

1/4 teaspoon pepper

Oil to deep fry

How to prepare:

1. In a large bowl, add in all the veggies, salt, chilli powder, garam masala, amchur, chaat masala, ginger garlic paste. Now add 1/4cup bread crumbs and give it a good mix.

2. In a small bowl, add the maida and little water to make a paste. Now make small balls of the mixture and dip in maida paste, and roll in the bread crumbs. Now deep fry in hot oil until golden brown or bake at 360 degrees F for 12 minutes.

3. Insert a toothpick to make a lollipop. Serve with tomato ketchup.

Mushroom Pakora

I call them gooey fungi pakoras. These mushroom pakoras just take about 10 minutes to cook. They are crispy on the first bite and soft on the inside. Mushroom pakoras are my family's favourite dish. You can also enjoy them as a tea-time snack.

Ingredients

1/2 cup gram flour

Pinch of baking soda

1/4 cup rice flour

Salt to taste

1/2 cup water

1/2 teaspoon garam masala

1/2 teaspoon ginger garlic paste

How to prepare:

In a mixing bowl, add gram flour, cup rice flour, chilli powder, garam masala, baking soda, water, and salt. Mix well to make a smooth batter that's a thin consistency. Dip the mushroom into the batter and coat it fully and fry until golden brown. Serve hot.

Gobi Padoka

Ingredients

1 1/2 cup gram flour

200 grams of parboiled cauliflower florets

2 teaspoon amchur

1/2 cup Water

2 cups oil

1/2 teaspoon of baking soda

2 teaspoon red chilli powder

Salt

1 teaspoon ginger garlic paste

How to prepare:

In a bowl, add the gram flour, red chili powder, amchur, baking soda, water, and salt. Mix them well and form a lump-free batter. In a pan, heat oil and deep fry the pakora until golden brown. Serve hot with mint chutney.

Indian Baked Tofu

This simple tofu dish is made by a marinade of south Indian flavours like curry powder (powdered curry leaves) which gives this dish a nice fragrance while it's baking.

Ingredients

140 oz extra firm tofu

3 tablespoon oil

1/2 teaspoon chilli powder

1 tablespoon curry powder

1 teaspoon ginger garlic paste

Salt as per taste

Pinch of turmeric

Juice of 1/2 lemon

How to prepare:

Drain the water completely from tofu and cut it into small cubes. In a bowl, add the ingredients from the marinade section and coat tofu cubes. Let it sit in the fridge for 30 minutes. Meanwhile, let us preheat the oven at 425 F for 15 minutes. Brush some oil onto a baking sheet and place the tofu cubes and bake for 30 minutes. Turn the cubes once in 5 minutes. To make them crispy, broil them for another 8 minutes.

***

Aloo 65

It got the number 65, from a restaurant in Hyderabad, India, where this dish was the 65th one, and they named it so. They are crispy soft fried aloo with south Indian masalas. Aloo 65 is dipped into mint chutney or even eaten alone.

Ingredients

5 parboiled, diced potatoes

3 tablespoon all-purpose flour

15 curry leaves

3 tablespoon corn flour

1 teaspoon chili powder

1/2 teaspoon coriander powder

1/2 teaspoon black pepper powder

1/2 teaspoon cumin powder

1 tablespoon lemon juice

2 teaspoon ginger garlic paste

1/2 teaspoon garam masala

Water to prepare the batter

Salt as required

Oil to deep fry

How to prepare:

In a bowl, add in all the ingredients except oil to prepare the batter. Now add the potatoes into the batter and coat them well. In a pan, heat the oil; once hot, add the coated potatoes into the oil and fry them until crispy and golden brown. Fry them evenly on all sides. Drain them onto a tissue to remove excess oil. Enjoy with mint chutney or tomato sauce.

Hara Bara Kabab

Hara bhara kababs are pan-fried veggie patties made with a mix of green peas, spinach, and potatoes. I loved these kebabs in restaurants; when my mom realized my interest, she learned how to make them and made these at home. By the way, here is my mom's recipe for you.

Ingredients

2 cups of fresh spinach

1 cup cold water

2 cups of hot water

200 grams boiled potatoes

150 grams boiled peas

1 chopped green chilies

4 tablespoon roasted gram flour

1 inch chopped ginger

1 teaspoon amchur powder

1 teaspoon chaat masala

1/4 teaspoon garam masala

Salt to taste

Oil for frying

8 cashews

How to prepare:

To blanch spinach, add them into hot boiled water for 2 minutes. Transfer them to cold water for a minute. Then chop the spinach. In a mortar and pestle, add the ginger, chilies and crush them. Take a bowl and add spinach, potatoes, peas, chilli, and ginger paste. Now with a masher, mash the kabab mixture. Add all the spice powders, salt, and gram flour. Mix them well. Make them into patties and pan-fry t golden brown and crispy. Serve hot with mint chutney.

Onion Rings

Ingredients

1 onion sliced into rings

1/2 cup of maida

20 chopped curry leaves

2 tablespoon corn flour

Salt to taste

1 finely chopped green chilies

1/2 cup water

1/2 teaspoon chilli powder

Oil for frying

1 cup corn flakes crumb

How to prepare:

In a bowl, add all the ingredients except oil and mix well to form lump-free batter. Now dip the onion ring into batter and coat well. Now drop the rings into corn flakes crumbs and coat well. Now do a double coating with batter and corn flakes crumb again. Fry until they are crispy and golden brown. Enjoy with hot Indian chai.

Corn Fritters

For me, the summer holidays remind me of a lot of corn. Nothing keeps me happier than corn. My mom cooked corn for an everyday snack. Corn fitters were the star among all. Enjoy it for snacks.

Ingredients

1/2 cup cornmeal

1/2 cup all-purpose flour

Salt

1 cup fresh corn

1/2 teaspoon chilli powder

15 curry leaves

Pinch of turmeric

I clove finely chopped garlic

1/2 cup soy milk

2 finely chopped green chilies

2 finely chopped onions

Pinch of baking powder

Peanut oil for frying

How to prepare:

In a bowl, add all the ingredients except soymilk and oil and combine well. Now add the milk and combine well to make a thick paste; add more milk if it looks dry. Heat up the oil in a pan over medium heat. Now, scoop about 2 tablespoons of batter into the hot oil. Cook them until golden brown for about 4-5 minutes. Flip frequently to ensure they are evenly cooked. Transfer them onto a paper towel to remove the oil. Enjoy!

Beetroot Cutlets

As a kid, I hated beetroot, and the only way my mom could feed me beets was with these yummy cutlets. I have some tips to make beetroot cutlets more tasty. First, squeeze out the excess water from the beetroot after grating. Add salt before squeezing to remove excess water. Add bread crumbs or corn starch to make them moisture-free. I have pan-fried cutlets, whereas you can deep fry them for kids.

Ingredients

250 grams of steamed and grated beetroot

275 grams of boiled and mashed potatoes

1/2 teaspoon Kashmiri red chilli powder

1/4 teaspoon turmeric

1 teaspoon fennel

1/2 teaspoon garam masala

1 teaspoon chaat masala

1 finely chopped green chili

1 teaspoon black salt

1 teaspoon amchur powder or lemon juice

1 teaspoon minced ginger

1/2 cup semolina

2 tablespoon rice flour

1/2 cup oil for pan frying

How to prepare:

In a bowl, add the beetroot, mashed potatoes, and all the ingredients except semolina and mix everything well. On a plate, add the roasted semolina. Now shape them into round patties and place them to coat them with semolina, dust off the excess semolina. Now brush the pan with oil and fry the cutlets till they turn crisp and golden brown. Serve hot with mint chutney.

Indian Pickles

Carrot Pickles

Unlike the vinegar pickles, Indian pickles are way different from them. A lot of spices go into Indian pickles to give them a taste that goes with rice or any Indian breads. This pickle is made by thinly slicing carrots and marinated with a spice mix and ensuring the flavours are rightly absorbed for 2 days.

Ingredients

5 tablespoon groundnut oil

1 1/2 cups thinly sliced carrots

2 inches of ginger juliennes

1 dried red chilli

1 tablespoon mustard seeds

1/4 teaspoon hing

15 curry leaves

2 teaspoon Kashmiri chilli powder

1/4 teaspoon turmeric powder

1 tablespoon salt

1/4 teaspoon roasted fenugreek seed powder

1/4 teaspoon roasted mustard powder

1 teaspoon white vinegar

The juice of 2 lemons

How to prepare:

1. First, in a pan, add 2 tablespoons of oil, ginger, carrot, and sauté them for a minute on medium flame. After 5 minutes, transfer them into a bowl and set them aside.

2. To the same oil, add the rest of the oil. Once hot, add the mustard seeds, red chilli, hing, and curry leaves. Further, add the turmeric, chilli powder, fenugreek powder, mustard powder, and lastly, salt. Give a good mix and switch off the flame.

3. Now, add the carrot and ginger. Lastly, add the vinegar and lemon juice. Give it a good mix. Once it is cooled, store it in a glass jar.

Lemon Pickle

The traditional lemon pickle is quite lengthy and time-consuming. This recipe here is an instant version. Lemon pickle is a burst of flavours, and it's so citrusy! Indians enjoy pickles with curd rice. Get your daily dose of vitamin C with this lemon pickle.

Ingredients

10 lemons

3 tablespoon kashmiri red chilli powder

1/4 teaspoon turmeric

1/4 teaspoon roasted fenugreek seed powder

2 teaspoon roasted mustard seed powder

1 tablespoon salt

1 teaspoon mustard seeds

1/4 cup ground nut oil

1/4 teaspoon hing

How to prepare:

1. First, in a vessel, add 4 cups of water and bring it to boil. Once it starts to boil, add the lemons and turn off the heat and let it rest covered for 5 minutes. Now, take out the lemons and pat dry. Make sure there's no moisture.

2. Chop them into 2 halves and set them aside. Add in the roasted mustard and fenugreek powder onto the lemons. Now, add the red chilli powder, salt, turmeric. Mix thoroughly.

3. In a pan, heat the oil, hing, and mustard seeds and let mustard seeds pop. Let it cool. Pour this tempering over pickle and mix well. Enjoy the instant lemon pickle with hot rice. Store it in a refrigerator and use it before 2 weeks.

Andra Avakaya

Although this pickle originates in the south Indian state of Andra Pradesh. It's popular all across India. Indians have a deep attachment to Andra pickles. This legendary mango pickle has its fan base that's incredible. Me, being Andrite, I get a lot of requests for this pickle during mango season. Enjoy this pickle along with sambar and hot rice, upma, or even with just hot rice.

Ingredients

1 and 1/2 kg raw mangoes

1/2 cup roasted mustard seed powder

1 tablespoon roasted fenugreek seed powder

2 teaspoons turmeric powder

2 cups Kashmiri red chilli powder

2 cups of salt

1/2 cups of peeled garlic pods

4 cups sesame oil

How to prepare:

1. On a kitchen towel, spread the pieces of mango and let them dry for 4 hours. In a pan, heat the oil. Once it's hot, turn off the heat and let it cool.

2. In a large bowl, add the mustard and fenugreek powder, turmeric, chilli, salt, garlic pods, 2 cups of cooled oil, and mix well. Transfer this into a glass jar and top it with the rest of the 2 cups of oil.

3. Cover the jar and keep it in strong sunlight for 4 days. Top with more oil into a jar, and make sure to cover the mangoes with oil.

Amla Pickle

The traditional amla pickle calls for sun drying the gooseberries for weeks to increase the shelf life of the pickle. Here we are using the steaming method to make instant pickle. Refrigerate the pickle and scoop out a few tablespoons for every day use. The amlas taste sour at first and sweeter at the end. Enjoy with hot rice.

Ingredients

7 gooseberries/amla

1/4 cup of mustard oil

Pinch of hing

2 teaspoon Kashmiri red chilli powder

1 teaspoon mustard seeds

1 teaspoon salt

1 teaspoon turmeric

1 teaspoon fenugreek seeds

1 teaspoon fennel seeds

2 teaspoon of mustard seeds

How to prepare:

1. Rinse the amlas and steam them for 10 minutes or cook until they open up. Now let it cool completely.

2. Chop the amlas into two halves and remove the seeds. Transfer them onto a plate and spread them to cool completely.

3. In a pan, dry roast the ingredients under masala paste until they turn golden. Now blend into a fine powder. Set this aside.

4. Heat the oil and add mustard seeds and hing. Let the mustard seeds pop. Turn off the heat. Add the steamed amlas and sauté for 2 minutes. Now, add the chilli powder, salt, and turmeric and mix them well. Now add the masala and mix well. And it's ready; enjoy this instant pickle with hot rice.

Mixed Vegetable Pickle

If you ever visit an Indian restaurant, you will most find at least 2 pickles on your table. Mostly, it would be mixed vegetable pickle since these vegetables are found in every season. For those off seasons when mangoes and lemons haven't hit the market yet, this tasty vegetable pickle comes handy.

Ingredients

150 grams of chopped cauliflower florets (small pieces)

60 grams of chopped carrot

1 cup aubergine (eggplant)

1 roughly chopped bell pepper

6 garlic cloves

3 sliced green chillies

1 teaspoon turmeric

Lemon juice of 3 lemons

1 tablespoon roasted mustard seed powder

1/2 teaspoon roasted fenugreek powder

3 tablespoon of flaky sea salt

125 ml of sunflower oil

2 teaspoon mustard seeds

1teaspoon cumin seeds

15 chopped curry leaves

2 dried Kashmiri chilles

How to prepare:

1. Add all the vegetables, including garlic, in a mixing

bowl. Add the lemon juice, mustard seed powder, chilli powder, fenugreek powder, turmeric, and salt into the bowl of vegetables. Mix well to combine.

2. Heat the pan over high flame, add 3 tablespoons of oil and add mustard seeds. Once they pop, turn the flame to medium and add the Kashmiri chillies, cumin seeds, and curry leaves. Once they turn fragrant, pour the rest of the oil and mix well. Now pour this oil over the vegetables. Mix well and make sure the vegetables are submerged in the oil.

3. Let it ferment for 3 days; stir it once in 8 hours. Store it in an airtight container and refrigerate. It will last for 3 months.

Indian Desserts

Kobari Louzu

Kobari louzu is a dessert from Andra that is made from freshly grated coconut and jaggery. My grandma always had these ready at home for us. This is my Grandmom's recipe for you which is simple and delicious.

Ingredients

2 cups of freshly grated coconut

1 1/2 cup jaggery

1 tablespoon coconut oil

1/2 cup water

4 fresh ground cardamom pods

How to prepare:

In a pan, add water and jaggery. Let it dissolve and bring it to a boil. Stir it frequently and allow this syrup to thicken for about 15 to 20 minutes. Now, add the grated coconut, cardamom powder, and stir till it becomes thick. It would take about 10 -1 5 minutes. Turn off the heat. Into a square mold and grease it with coconut oil, and pour this mixture immediately. Spread this out and let it cool. Cut into any shapes and enjoy.

Pineapple Kesari

Pineapple kesari is a sweet made of semolina and pineapples. The flavors like natural fruit sugar and sourness along with the fragrance of pineapple will make this dish so special. Unlike the monotonous sugary taste, I highly recommend you use coarse or medium-sized semolina for this recipe. It is eaten for breakfast or as a dessert.

Ingredients

1 cup semolina

1 teaspoon coconut oil

1/2 cup non-dairy butter or coconut oil

1 cup chopped pineapple

1 cup unrefined cane sugar

3 cups of water

1/4 teaspoon cardamom powder

Mixed nuts for garnish

Finely chopped pineapple for garnish

1 tablespoon coconut oil

10 cashews

2 tablespoon raisins

How to prepare:

1. In a pan, heat 1 tablespoon coconut oil and roast the cashews and raisins and keep them aside.

2. In a large pan, add 1/4 cup of sugar and 3 cups of water and combine well. Adjust the sugar if pineapples are sour. Cook covered for 3 minutes; by now the pineapples should be soft.

3. Add the semolina and keep stirring to make sure there are no lumps. Once the semolina has absorbed the water, add the sugar. Once it melts, add non-dairy butter and mix well. Cover and cook for 5 minutes on low heat.

4. Lastly, add cashews, raisins, and cardamom powder and mix well. Garnish with nuts and pineapple.

Ragi Biscuits

These are probably the healthiest biscuits one could come across. Ragi is nothing but finger millet. These days, most of the biscuits are made of refined all-purpose flour. I think ragi biscuits are unsung heroes. I'm fortunate enough to have grown up eating these super-nutritious biscuits. Try these biscuits for your kids.

Ingredients

3/4 cup of finger millet flour (ragi flour)

1/2 cup jaggery powder

1/4 cup wheat flour

6 tablespoon olive oil

1/2 cup warm water

1 tablespoon baking powder

1 flax egg (1 tablespoon of flax seed powder mixed with 3 tablespoons of water and soaked for 20 minutes)

How to prepare:

1. First, preheat the oven to 350 degrees F or at 180 degrees Celsius. In a mixing bowl, sieve together ragi and wheat flour. Now add in the jaggery, baking powder, flax egg, and mix well with your fingers. Now add the oil and mix well to make the dough. Add a few tablespoons of water if needed.

2. Divide the dough into equal balls and place them on a baking tray. Press the ball to flatten and bake for about 12-15 minutes. Remove when edges turn brown. Store the biscuits in an airtight container. Enjoy with tea.

Gajar Ka Halwa

Gajar ka halwa is a simple carrot pudding made with grated carrots, nuts, and sugar syrup. It's often eaten along with ice cream. Trust me, it tastes fabulous.

Ingredients

1 1/2 pounds grated carrot

2 tablespoon sesame oil

1/2 cup sliced almonds

1/2 cup of cashews and pistachios

1 teaspoon cardamom powder

1 cup unrefined cane sugar

1 cup raw cashews

How to prepare:

1. In a blender, add the cashews and 3 cups of water and blend to make a smooth paste. In a large wide pan, heat 1 tablespoon oil and add the almonds and nuts and sauté

for a minute.

2. Add in the carrots and crushed cardamom and sauté for 2 minutes. Add in the cashew milk. Cook over medium heat and stir occasionally until the milk has been absorbed into cashews, which would take about 15- 20 minutes.

3. On high heat, keep stirring the carrots as they may stick to the pan. Now add the sugar and 1 tablespoon oil and stir until the sugar has dissolved.

4. Now, you can cook your halwa for longer or turn off the heat. It will have the texture of pudding. Enjoy it warm or cold. Garnish with sliced almonds.

Date Roll

This simple dish comes in handy for those impromptu guests or parties. This dish is healthy and less laborious and will be ready in less than 20 minutes. All you need is 3 ingredients and you are good to go.

Ingredients

250 grams of seedless dates

200 grams of mixed and chopped peanuts, cashews, walnuts, almonds

Vegan butter (Faba butter) or coconut oil

How to prepare:

1. In a grinder, grind the dates into a smooth paste. Add vegan butter or coconut oil to get it smooth.

2. In a pan, roast the mixed nuts and grind them as well. Add some vegan butter to get a crumbly texture.

3. Now, on a plastic surface, put the date mixture and spread it out a flat and half-inch thick. Add the nuts mixture on top of the dates mixture and cover it. Give the mixture a gentle press to stick it. Now roll out to make rolls.

4. Then let it rest in the freezer for 10 minutes. Cut the rolls by slicing into half-inch thick chunks.

Moong Dal Halwa

Moong dal halwa is made by soaking split yellow mung lentils cooked with sugar syrup and topped with nuts. This north Indian dish is made for special occasions and is one of the most scrumptious sweets I have come across.

Ingredients

1 cup moong dal

3/4 cup coconut oil

2 cups of water

1 cup unrefined cane sugar

1/4 teaspoon cardamom powder

Crushed mixed nuts like almonds, cashews, pistachios for

garnish

How to prepare:

1. In a pan, dry roast the moong dal until golden brown for 8-10 minutes. Add in the water and stir. Cook covered with a pressure valve for 20 minutes on high heat. Quick-release the pressure and add the sugar, oil, and cardamom to this and mix well.

2. The dal might look dry; it's okay since the dal will absorb the oil. Once it absorbs, keep stirring the dal for 10 minutes, scraping the bottom regularly. Cook until the oil oozes out of on top and separates at the bottom. That's perfect. Now transfer into a serving bowl. Garnish with nuts and enjoy.

Kheer

If there's any dessert that's truly universal, it has to be kheer. This unites three traditional cuisines - Indian, west, and middle eastern. It's called payasam or phirni and many names all across India. There can't be any festival without kheer. It's a dish that's a mix of religions and traditions. Both Hindus and Muslims have their kheer recipes figured out. Try this Indian rice pudding.

Ingredients

3 cups of almond milk

4 tablespoon unrefined cane sugar

1 cup of oat milk

2 tsp cardamom powder

¼ cup basmati rice

A few strands of saffron

Mixed nuts like cashews, raisins, almonds, and pistachios

How to prepare:

Let the basmati rice soak while we heat the almond and oat milk. Soak saffron in a small bowl with 3 tablespoons of water. In a pot, bring the milk to boil and simmer. Drain the water and add rice to the milk. Cook for 10 minutes or until rice softens. Add the cardamom, sugar, saffron water along with saffron strands. Cook for 10 more minutes in low heat. Kheer can be thick or watery, whichever consistency you like. Adjust sweetness and add the mixed nuts and stir. Serve hot or chilled.

Lauki Halwa

I haven't met anyone who doesn't hate bottle gourd. Indians turned the boring bottle gourd into a delicious dessert. Almost every wedding I attended had lauki halwa on their menu. Serve this lauki halwa to your guests without revealing this star ingredient until compliments start pouring in.

Ingredients

3 tablespoons of coconut oil

2 1/2 cups of grated bottle gourd (lauki)

1/4 cup mixed nuts

2 cups of coconut milk

1/4 cup unrefined cane sugar

1 tablespoon of cardamom powder

1/2 cup semolina

How to prepare:

In a pan, roast the semolina until golden brown and transfer into a bowl. Heat the oil and roast the mixed nuts for a minute. Transfer them to a bowl. Now add in the grated lauki and cook covered until soft for 10 minutes on low flame. Stir often. Now, add the coconut milk and combine and cook for 10 more minutes. Lastly, add the sugar and cardamom powder and mix well. Serve hot or chilled.

Dry Fruit Date Burfi

If you ever visit Indian sweet shops, you will most likely come across this burfi being sold in all most every sweet shop. It is that popular and tasty. This recipe has various kinds of seeds and nuts. The best part is that it is devoid of sugar and uses only dates for a sweet flavour.

Ingredients

1 cup pitted dates

1 tablespoon coconut oil

1 tablespoon poppy seeds

1/4 cup dry grated coconut

1/4 cup chopped almonds

1 tablespoon sesame seeds

1/4 cup chopped cashews

1/4 cup chopped pistachios

1/4 cup chopped walnuts

2 tablespoon raisins

1/4 teaspoon cardamom powder

2 tablespoon watermelon seeds

How to prepare:

1. Heat the 1 tablespoon coconut oil and roast the sesame seeds and poppy seeds until golden brown. Now roast 1/4 cup dry coconut until it slightly changes colour. Further, add the almonds, cashews, pistachios, walnuts, and raisins. Roast for 5 minutes on low flame or until they are crunchy. Now add the crushed dates, 1/4 teaspoon cardamom powder, and mix well.

2. Continue cooking on medium flame and smash the dates with the masher. Turn off the heat and spread it in a square mold, and allow it to cool. Now cut into thick

chunks once it's completely set. Store it in an airtight container. These burfis will last for a month.

Kesar Badam Kulfi

Kulfi is a dense ice cream made of condensed milk that is left unwhipped. It is frozen at temperatures higher than the refrigerator. It is called matka kulfi (earthen pot kulfi). Kulfi molds are kept in an earthen pot with an ice salt mixture to freeze to achieve the dense, soft ice cream. Since we can't make kulfi so authentically, we will have to keep kulfis out of the refrigerator for 2 minutes before serving for that softer state.

Ingredients

1 can (13 .5 oz) of full-fat coconut milk

3 tablespoons of water

1/2 teaspoon saffron strands

80 grams of unrefined cane sugar

1/2 teaspoon cardamom powder

1/3 cup of ground raw cashews

1/4 teaspoon sea salt

1 tablespoon cornstarch

1/2 cup of chopped mixed nuts like almonds and pistachios.

How to prepare:

1. Heat the pan and add water and saffron and simmer for 5 minutes. Add the sugar and let it dissolve, and bring it to a boil. In a bowl, add the cashews, 1/2 cup coconut milk, cornstarch, and keep it ready.

2. Now add this into the sugar syrup along with salt and cardamom, bring it to boil, and turn off the heat. Now add the remaining milk and combine well. Adjust sugar. Lastly, add this mixture into pop molds and freeze. Serve it with mixed nuts.

Ragi Kilsa

Ragi kilsa is a sweet made of finger millet, jaggery, and coconut. Ragi kilsa means the milk extract of the finger millet. This dish hails from the southern state of Karnataka. It is common among Kannadigas to consume this during the summer. It is believed to cool our body.

Ingredients

1 cup finger millets (soaked for 8 hours)

1/2 cup fresh grated coconut

1 cup jaggery

2 cardamom

1 tablespoon of coconut oil for greasing

2 cups of water

How to prepare:

1. First, grind the soaked finger millet and coconut into a fine paste. To a hot pan, add some water, jaggery and let it dissolve completely dissolve on medium flame. Once you see bubbles, add the millet coconut paste. Stir to make sure there are no lumps. Let it cook for good 30 minutes on low flame. Stir frequently in between.

2. Once it thickens and leaves the sides of the pan. Turn off the heat. On to a plate, brush coconut oil and spread this mixture evenly. Cut into the desired shape. Serve once it cools down.

Minapa Suniundalu

This delicacy made of urad dal is my grandam's favourite. This is made of Urad dal and hails from Andra Pradesh. It is consumed almost every day because they have an impressively long shelf life. They can last up to 10 days. They were packed for our trips for the same reason.

Ingredients

1 cup unrefined cane sugar

1 1/2 cup dry roasted urad dal until golden (for 15- 20 minutes)

1 tablespoon dry roasted rice

1/2 cup canola oil or sesame oil

How to prepare:

1. In a blender, add in the roasted rice and urad dal along with sugar and blend into a fine powder.

2. In a pan, heat the oil, and once hot, turn off the heat. In a bowl, add the powder, adjust the sugar, now slowly pour the oil and combine everything. Rub some oil onto your palms to roll the mixture into round balls.

Rava Ladoo

Rava ladoo is a south Indian dessert made of roasted semolina, coconut, nuts, and sugar. These are made during festivals and are common return gifts to guests. They have a crunchy texture with a heavenly aroma.

They have a shelf life of 1 month, which is great.

Ingredients

1 cup semolina

3/4 cup unrefined cane sugar

1/4 cup desiccated coconut

1/4 cup sesame oil or canola oil

5 crushed cardamom pods

15 broken cashews

15 raisins

How to prepare:

1. In a pan, dry roast the semolina and coconut for 7-8 minutes on a medium flame. Stir frequently and let it cool.

2. In a grinder, add the sugar and cardamoms and grind to make a fine paste. Now, to the same grinder, add the semolina to make a fine powder. If it's too coarse, the mixture might not bind. Transfer this into a large bowl.

3. In a pan, heat the oil and add the cashews and raisins and fry until golden. Now add this to the semolina bowl and mix well. Now press the mixture between your palms to make round balls. Store them for up to 15 days in an airtight container.

Falooda

Falooda is a layered dessert drink from Persia that's popular all over India, especially during summers. There are several layers like rose syrup, sweet basil seeds, vermicelli almond milk, and mixed nuts. Falooda can be enjoyed with or without ice cream. You will find falooda sev (noodles) easily in any Indian store.

Ingredients

5 tablespoons of falooda sev = 12 tablespoons of cooked falooda sev

2 cups of water

6 tablespoon of soaked basil seeds or chia seeds (20 minutes in water)

6 tablespoons of rose syrup

4 scoops of vegan vanilla ice cream

4 cups of chilled almond milk

12 sliced pistachios

12 chopped cashews

12 sliced almonds

12 raisins

How to prepare:

1. Cook falooda sev according to instructions. Some require cooking, whereas some just need to be soaked in

warm water. Boil the falooda sev in the water on medium flame until soft, just like you do for noodles. Strain it and let it cool.

2. Take 4 tall glasses or bowls. Fill the ingredients into each glasses. Add 1.5 to 2 tablespoons of rose syrup into each glass and then 2 to 3 tablespoons of falooda sev with 1 cup milk and top it with 1 scoop of ice cream.

3. Finally, garnish with nuts and raisins. Serve immediately, mix the rose syrup in the bottom with a spoon and enjoy.

Mango Kulfi

Indian summers call for mangoes and kulfis. Indian mangoes are one of the finest mangoes in the world. For this recipe, use only Indian mangoes. In my opinion, you haven't tasted real mango until you have had Indian mangoes. Mango kulfi is made using mango pulp and fresh almond milk, and cashews with sugar. You will love it.

Ingredients

1 cup of soaked cashews (30 minutes)

3/4 cup almond milk

1/2 cup unrefined cane sugar

2 1/2 cups of fresh mango pulp

1 teaspoon vanilla extract

1 teaspoon cardamom powder

How to prepare:

Add in all the ingredients in a blender and blend until smooth. Pour this mixture into popsicle molds with popsicle sticks and freeze. Unmold it by dipping in slightly warm water, pop it out, and enjoy!

Besan Ladoo

Besan ladoo is a sweet made of chickpea flour, cashews, and sugar. It just takes 15 minutes and has a shelf life of

2 weeks. It can be packed for trips as well. You can add roasted semolina for the crunch or simply keep the gram flour coarse. Besan ladoo is our favourite dinner time dessert at our home.

Ingredients

2 cup coarse gram flour (Besan)

1 cup unrefined cane sugar or jaggery

1/2 cup vegan butter

4 cardamom pods

10 tablespoon chopped cashews

2 tablespoon melon seeds

How to prepare:

1. In a large pan, heat 1/2 cup vegan butter and 2 cup gram flour. Roast them on low flame. Add more vegan

butter if the mixture looks dry. After 20 minutes, you will see gram flour releasing butter/oil. Roast until flour turns golden brown; it might take about 10 more minutes. Let it cool.

2. Meanwhile, roast the melon seeds and cashews on low flame until crunchy. Add them to flour. In a blender, add the sugar and cardamom pods and blend them into a fine powder. Add this to the slightly warm gram flour. Roll them into balls to make ladoos.

Amla Murabba

Amla is Indian gooseberry; this dish is made by cooking Indian gooseberries in sugar syrup. Further, add saffron, black pepper, black salt, and cardamom to enhance flavours. Amla is known to boost our immune system and are in abundance during the winter. Enjoy this sweet, tangy pickle. Enjoy it alone or with bread or on a salad. It has a shelf life of up to 1 year when stored in the refrigerator.

Ingredients

500 grams of Indian gooseberry

1/4 teaspoon black pepper powder

5 crushed green cardamoms

1/4 teaspoon saffron

1/4 teaspoon alum

750 grams of cane sugar

1/2 teaspoon black salt

How to prepare:

1. To a pan with boiling water, add the amlas and boil for 15 minutes, or until soft. Turn off the heat. Now, pierce amlas with a fork so that the sugar syrup is absorbed by the amlas.

2. In a pan, prepare sugar syrup with 3 cups of water. Boil for 15 minutes on medium flame. Once the syrup is as

thick as honey, add the black pepper, cardamom, alum, black salt, and saffron. Mix well and serve.

Bread Halwa

Bread halwa is nothing but pudding made of bread. This is my go-to dessert during my college days since it's so economical and easy to make. Trust me, it just takes 15 minutes to get this dish ready. You can also add some ice cream on top to give a food coma to your guests.

Ingredients

7 slices of any bread

1 ¼ cup almond milk

1/3 cup + 2 teaspoons coconut oil

1/4 teaspoon rose water (optional)

2 teaspoons raisins

2 teaspoons cashews

1/2 cup sugar (1/3 cup agave nectar)

2 tablespoons grated coconut

2 tablespoon crushed cardamom

How to prepare:

1. In a pan, add 2 tablespoons coconut oil and sauté the cashews and raisins until golden brown and set aside. To the same pan, add 1/3 cup coconut oil and once hot, add bread crumbs and sauté over medium heat for 10 minutes. Transfer on to a plate.

2. Meanwhile, heat a pan and add the almond milk and sugar and bring it to a boil. Add in the bread crumbs, cardamom, and rose water and cook covered on low heat for 5 minutes. Once the almond milk is absorbed by the bread crumbs, cook over medium heat while stirring frequently. Once the mixture pulls off from the sides, turn off the heat and add the cashews and raisins. Serve hot!

Alasanda Vada (bobarlu vada)

Alasanda vada, also known as bobarlu vada, is made of black-eyed beans, onion, chillies, and curry leaves, along with Indian spices into fritters. Vada is nothing but fritters. Alasanda or bobarlu is black-eyed beans. This dish hails from Andra Pradesh, a southern state in India. These vadas are power-packed with nutrition.

Ingredients

1 cup black-eyed beans (soaked for 4 hours)

1 chopped onion

15 chopped curry leaves

1/2 teaspoon red chilli powder

1-inch minced ginger

4 finely chopped garlic cloves

1 teaspoon cumin seeds

1 teaspoon turmeric powder

Sunflower oil for frying

1 teaspoon turmeric

How to prepare:

1. In a grinder, grind the beans into a coarse mixture, add

water as needed. Add all the ingredients into a bowl along with a bean mixture. Combine well, adjust salt and spices as needed.

2. In a pan, heat the oil for frying. You can roast them in the pan as we do for cutlets. Scoop out some mixture and press it to make flat round fritters and add into the oil. Make sure to flip and cook evenly on both sides. Vada should be cooked on low to medium flame until golden brown. Serve them hot with coconut chutney.

Mangalore Bun

Mangalore bun is a fried bread that has a mild sweet taste and fruity flavour, which comes from ripened bananas. It's made of mashed bananas, sugar, and flour. It is left to ferment to get that chewy texture. These sweet banana pooris hail from Mangalore, Karnataka.

Ingredients

1 cup all-purpose flour (maida)

6-8 ripened bananas

1 cup wheat flour

1/2 teaspoon baking soda

1 teaspoon carom seeds

Salt to taste

2 teaspoons oil for dough

Oil for frying

2-4 spoons of unrefined cane sugar

How to prepare:

1. Mash bananas to make a puree. Mix all the ingredients in a bowl along with banana puree. Knead the dough by adding 2 tablespoons of oil. Make sure the dough is soft and not stiff. If the dough is sticky, add some wheat flour.

2. Let the dough sit covered for 5 hours or overnight. Once the dough rises, divide into equal balls and roll them with a rolling pin. Flatten them but not too thin.

2. In a pan, heat the oil to fry these buns. Flip it once it's puffy and fry until it's brown.

Aloo Samosa

Samosa is a fried snack with stuffing like potato, onion, and peas. Here we are learning about Punjabi aloo samosa. Samosa is one of the most popular street food in India. It is also popular in the Middle East and Asia. It originated in the Middle East and was bought by merchants to India. Enjoy this with a hot cup of chai.

Ingredients

2 teaspoon oil

1 teaspoon cumin

4 boiled and mashed potatoes

1/2 teaspoon fennel

1/2 teaspoon crushed coriander seeds

1 inch finely chopped ginger

1 finely chopped chilli

1/2 teaspoon coriander powder

1/2 teaspoon amchur

1/4 teaspoon cumin powder

1/2 teaspoon chilli powder

1/2 teaspoon garam masala

3/4 teaspoon salt

2 tablespoons finely chopped coriander leaves

Water to seal samosa

Oil for deep frying

2 cups of all-purpose flour

1/4 teaspoon carom seeds

1/2 teaspoon salt

1/2 cup water

1/4 cup oil

How to prepare:

Take a small ball of dough and roll it into an oval shape.
Cut it in between for 2 equal portions. Grease with some
water and make a cone. Stuff the filling into a cone.
Grease the edges with water and seal them by pressing
firmly. In a pan with hot oil, deep fry the samosas on low
flame for 15 minutes until golden brown. Flip them in
between to cook evenly. Or you can bake them at 365
degrees Fahrenheit for 40 minutes. Enjoy aloo samosa
with mint chutney.

Ambode Vada

Ambode is a spicy, flavourful fritter from Karnataka. It is made with soaked chana dal and dill leaves. Authentic ambode is made with dill leaves, but you can substitute coriander leaves, curry leaves, or mint leaves. One cannot stop with one vada. Enjoy this tea-time snack.

Ingredients

1 cup chana dal (soaked 4 hours or overnight)

3 tablespoon rice flour

1 sprig chopped dill leaves

1/4 cup chopped coriander leaves

1 finely chopped onion

1 inch finely chopped ginger

7 finely chopped green chillies

Salt as required

Oil for deep frying

How to prepare:

Grind the soaked chana dal into a coarse paste without water. In a bowl, add all the ingredients along with the chana paste. Combine them well. Make small dough balls and press them to flatten them. In a hot pan with oil, fry the fritters over medium heat until golden brown. Enjoy!

Masala Chickpeas

These masala chickpeas are a great snack to munch on. Cooked chickpeas are marinated with spices and flour and baked for a crispy snack. These chickpeas are combined with onion, coriander, tomato, and a dash of lemon juice.

Ingredients

3 cups of cooked chickpeas (boiled or steamed until soft) — may use canned, too

2 tablespoons of sunflower oil

1 teaspoon chilli powder

Salt as per taste

3 tablespoons rice flour

1 1/2 teaspoon garlic powder

1 1/2 teaspoons garam masala

1/2 teaspoon amchur powder

1/2 teaspoon turmeric

3 tablespoons chickpea flour

How to prepare:

1. Preheat the oven to 425 degrees Fahrenheit. Remove the water and add chickpeas to the bowl. Add all the ingredients and combine well to coat. Add less salt if

using canned ones. Add oil and chickpea flour, rice flour, and mix well.

2. Spray some water to stick the flour to peas. Spread them on the baking sheet. Bake for 20 minutes. Flip and move them once in 5 minutes. Bake for 10 minutes or until crisp.

3. Let them cool to store them in an airtight jar. Add chaat masala or finely chopped onions, tomatoes, coriander, and lemon juice, and enjoy.

Onion Pakoda

In my house, any rainy day calls for an onion pakoda. Rainy weather makes me crave onion pakoda. The best thing is they are made in a jiffy. Enjoy these crispy onion fritters with a hot cup of chai.

Ingredients

1 1/2 cups of gram flour

1/2 cup rice flour

4 finely chopped green chillis

3 sliced onions

2 tablespoons freshly crushed coriander seeds

15 chopped curry leaves

Pinch of baking soda

Salt to taste

Oil for deep frying

How to prepare:

1. Add the vegetables and spices and give them a mix. Now add the flour and salt, baking soda. Combine to achieve a crumbly texture. Add a few drops of water and mix well to form a hard batter.

2. In a pan with hot oil, fry the pakodas by dropping the batter with your fingers. Make sure to drop small fritters. Cook them on medium heat, flip them to cook evenly until golden brown. Transfer them on tissue paper. Enjoy them hot.

Roasted Makhana

Makhana is an Indian term for lotus seed or fox nut. These simple roasted fox nuts are my nephew's favourite. This is his snack lunch box staple for school. It's a light and healthy snack and a great choice for health freaks.

Ingredients

2 cups of foxnuts

Salt to taste

2 teaspoons oil

1/2 teaspoon red chilli powder

1/4 teaspoon turmeric powder

1/2 teaspoon chaat masala

How to prepare:

1. In a wide pan, heat 1 teaspoon oil and foxnuts. Roast them on low flame until crunchy. It will take about 10 minutes for them to roast completely. Transfer them onto the plate. Heat 1 teaspoon of oil in the same pan. Add turmeric, salt, chilli powder, and add makhanas to the pan. Give them a good toss and turn off the flame. Sprinkle some chaat masala. Mix well and store in an airtight jar. Enjoy the crispy, crunchy makhana as a movie-time snack.

Cut Mirchi Bajji

Take a walk through south Indian streets in the evening, and you will smell the frying mirchi bajjis around the corner. Go to any south Indian wedding, and mirchi bajji is a staple dish. This recipe is from Andra Pradesh, named cut mirchi bajji due to the filling that goes inside. Enjoy mirchi bajji on cozy rainy days.

Ingredients

2 cups of gram flour

10 large green chillies

1/4 teaspoon carom seeds

2 tablespoon rice flour

1/4 teaspoon baking soda

3/4 cup of water

1 tablespoon oil

1/2 teaspoon salt

Oil for frying

1 tablespoon besan powder

1 teaspoon cumin powder

2 tablespoons of lemon juice

1 finely chopped onion

2 tablespoons finely chopped coriander

10 teaspoons of lemon juice

How to prepare:

1. Slit and deseed the green chilis. In a bowl, add all the ingredients for the batter and mix well to make the lump-free batter. Adjust water to form a thick batter.

2. Meanwhile, heat the pan with oil. Now add 1 tablespoon of hot oil into the batter and combine well to achieve a smooth batter. Combine all the ingredients under cumin filling in a bowl.

3. Fill the slit chillis with this filling. Now dip them into the batter and coat them well and fry in hot oil over medium heat until golden. Transfer onto tissue, now slit them add top with onions, coriander, and add lemon juice

on top. Enjoy hot!

Indian Chaats

Shakarkandi Chaat

Shakarkandi is the Indian term for sweet potato. Sweet potatoes are widely consumed across India. They are roasted, boiled, or made into curries in India. This recipe is from my beach visit to Marina Beach, Chennai. A vendor made these yummy sweet potatoes. I couldn't stop myself from asking her the recipe.

Ingredients

2 cups boiled or steamed sweet potatoes

1/4 teaspoon black pepper powder

1/2 teaspoon amchur powder

Roasted cumin seeds (optional)

1/2 teaspoon chaat masala(optional)

1 teaspoon lemon juice

Black salt as required

How to prepare:

In a bowl, add the sweet potatoes and chop them into small cubes and add all the ingredients, and adjust them as per your taste. Mix them well and serve.

Fruit Veggie Chaat

This simple chaat is a mix of vegetables and fruits with

black salt, cumin powder, chaat masala, and finally topped with peanuts for a crunchy twist.

Ingredients

1 chopped carrot

1 chopped cucumber

1 chopped apple

1 chopped pineapple

1 cup pomegranate seeds

3 tablespoons peanuts

1/4 cup green grapes

1 teaspoon chaat masala

1 teaspoon cumin powder

1/4 teaspoon black salt

1 teaspoon lemon juice

How to prepare:

In a large bowl, add all the ingredients except peanuts and toss them to combine. Add more chaat masala if using regular salt. Add peanuts before serving. Enjoy this simple fruit vegetable salad.

Corn Chaat

My brother was very fond of corn. So my mom was always trying new recipes to make it delicious. He would buy every kind of corn that's on the shelf in the store. So, this recipe is one among all the corn recipes my mom made. I'm sure you will like it.

Ingredients

1 medium boiled or steamed corn cob

1 finely chopped tomato

1 finely chopped green chilli

1 finely chopped onion

1 teaspoon lemon juice

1/2 teaspoon cumin powder

1/4 teaspoon chilli powder

1 tablespoon chopped coriander

Salt to taste

How to prepare:

Remove the kernels off the cob with hands or a knife.

In a medium-sized bowl, add kernels and all the ingredients. Combine well. You can also add soaked or boiled channa dal. Enjoy!

Peanut Chaat

These simple peanuts are ridiculously quick and tasty. All it takes is seven ingredients and five minutes. This salad is tangy and spicy with full of Indian flavours. Enjoy this snack for parties.

Ingredients

1 cup salted peanuts

2 finely chopped and deseeded tomatoes

1/2 chopped onion

Half lemon

1 teaspoon chaat masala

1 finely chopped chilli

2 tablespoons chopped coriander

How to prepare:

In a bowl, toss all the chopped vegetables and peanuts. Squeeze the lemon juice and mix well, sprinkle chaat masala and mix well. Serve immediately.

Puffed Rice Mixture

The puffed rice mixture is a popular street snack all across India. There are many different ways to make this snack. In north India, they add mashed potatoes, sugar syrup, and papdi. Some also add cornflakes or channa dal. Here is a basic version of the mixture.

Ingredients

3 cups of puffed rice

1 finely chopped green chilli

1 finely chopped onion

1/3 cup roasted peeled peanuts

2 tablespoons coriander leaves

1 teaspoon red chilli powder

1 deseeded and chopped tomato

Salt to taste

1 lemon

1 teaspoon chat masala

How to prepare:

In a large mixing bowl, add all the ingredients and mix well. Finally, squeeze lemon juice and serve immediately.

Masala Papad

Masala papad is the most popular restaurant appetizer for Indians. When at restaurants, masala papad is a mandatory dish. It's so simple and yet so yummy. It takes five minutes to make this. You can buy the papad with carom seeds in many Indian stores.

Ingredients

4 fried or roasted papad

1 finely chopped onion

1/2 cup finely chopped tomato

1 finely chopped green chilli

Salt to taste

2 tablespoon chopped coriander

1 teaspoon chaat masala

2 tablespoon lemon juice

1/4 teaspoon red chilli powder

How to prepare:

Keep papad on a serving plate. Add the rest of all the ingredients to a mixing bowl. And mix them all. Top papads with this mixture while serving; serve immediately before papads become soggy.

Indian Salads and Side Dishes

Indian Bean Salad

This salad is made of black eye beans; it is popularly called lobia chaat. It's spicy, sweet, and tangy. This salad calls for soaked black-eyed beans, potatoes, and herbs, along with Indian spices.

Ingredients

2 cups soaked black eye beans for 3 hours

5 peeled potatoes

1 1/2 cups water

Spices

1 teaspoon coriander powder

1 1/2 salt to taste

1 teaspoon amchur

1 teaspoon roasted cumin powder

1/4 teaspoon cayenne

1/4 teaspoon black salt

1/8 teaspoon black pepper

1 minced green chillis

1/4 cup chopped onions

1/2 cup chopped coriander

3 tablespoon mint chutney (look under Indian chutneys)

1/4 cup tamarind pulp mixed with 2 tablespoons of cane sugar

2 tablespoons lemon juice

How to prepare:

In a pressure cooker, cook the black eye beans and potatoes along with water for 10 minutes on high flame. Let the pressure release naturally. Then, take out the potatoes and cool them. Chop the potatoes and set them aside. Add the spices into the pot of beans. In a bowl, combine all the dressing ingredients. Add this to beans and mix well. Add the potatoes and mix well. Let it sit for 5 minutes. Serve warm.

Kosambri

This authentic salad hails from Karnataka. This is served for every wedding and any functions. It is made of soaked moong lentils, freshly grated coconut, and veggies like carrots and cucumbers and topped with pomegranate.

Ingredients

For the salad:

1 grated carrot

1/2 cup moong dal (30 minutes)

1/4 grated coconut

1 grated cucumber

1 finely chopped green chilies

1 tablespoon chopped coriander leaves

1/2 tablespoon lime juice

For garnish:

4 tablespoons pomegranate seeds

Salt to taste

For the dressing:

1 teaspoon urad dal

1/2 teaspoon mustard seeds

Pinch of hing

10 curry leaves

1 teaspoon oil

How to prepare:

In a mixing bowl, add the strained moong dal and

everything under the list of salad. Mix well. Now, let's add the tempering. To a hot pan, add oil, mustard seeds, urad dal, curry leaves, and hing, and fry for few seconds. Add this tempering to the mixed salad. Mix well and garnish with pomegranate. Enjoy!

Royal Fruit Chaat

This bowl has an ample assortment of fruits like apples, pineapples, papaya, bananas, and grapes. The water-filled cucumbers add crunch to this salad. Date syrup and tamarind paste will give an Indian spin to this salad. You can also substitute tamarind pulp with lemon juice and dates syrup with maple syrup.

Ingredients

1 cup of chopped apple cubes

1 cup of chopped papaya cubes

3/4 cup of chopped pineapple cubes

1 cup of sliced bananas

1/2 cup of black grapes, cut into halves.

1/4 cup of Indian gooseberry

1 tablespoon green chutney

1/2 cup of sliced cucumbers

1/2 tablespoon of dates syrup

1 tablespoon finely chopped coriander leaves

1/2 tablespoon tamarind paste

Pinch of turmeric

1/2 teaspoon roasted cumin powder

1/4 teaspoon black salt

1 teaspoon Indian chaat masala

1/4 teaspoon chilli powder

Salt to taste

How to prepare:

In a large bowl, add in all the fruits. Now add in the tamarind paste, dates syrup, chilli powder, chaat masala, turmeric, salt, and cumin powder. Toss them well, add in the bananas, cucumbers, and coriander leaves and toss them and enjoy.

Kachumber Salad Dip

Kachumber salad is a simple salad made of freshly chopped onions, cucumbers, tomatoes, salt, cayenne, and lemon dressing. You can also add radishes and carrots, and vinegar or yogurt for dressing. Serve this as a dip with chips, tacos, burritos, or in a wrap.

Ingredients

1 tomato

1 cucumber

Chopped coriander

1 medium onion

1 teaspoon cayenne

Fresh lemon juice

Add your favourite beans or peas (Boiled)

Roasted peanuts

How to prepare:

Finely chop all the ingredients and toss them. Add lemon juice and coriander and top with peanuts. Mix well and enjoy.

Phaal Chaat

Phaal is an Indian term for the fruit. This fruit salad has

soft bananas and strawberries, citrusy orange and lemon, crunchy apples and pears, along with an Indian spice mix. Enjoy this fruit bowl for breakfast.

Ingredients

1 sliced banana

1 chopped apple

1 chopped orange

1 chopped pear

5 chopped strawberries

1/4 teaspoon crushed pepper

1/4 teaspoon salt

1/2 teaspoon chaat masala

5 mint leaves

1/4 teaspoon cumin powder

1 teaspoon lemon juice

How to prepare:

In a bowl, add all the ingredients and mix well and serve chilled.

Chutta Moong Dal

Chutta moong dal is an authentic side dish from Gujarati cuisine. It's prepared with soaked, husked moong dal. Basic tempering goes into this dish. My mom adds steamed cabbage to it when I get health-conscious. It is usually served with gujarati kadhi or in thali as a side dish.

Ingredients

1 cup soaked yellow moong dal (for 30 minutes)

2 tablespoons groundnut oil

1/2 teaspoon cumin seeds

1/2 teaspoon mustard seeds

1 dried red chill

Pinch of hing

1/2 teaspoon red chilli powder

1/2 teaspoon minced ginger and chilli

Chopped coriander leaves

2 tablespoons of lemon juice

How to prepare:

In a thick bottomed pan, heat the oil. Once hot, add the
cumin and mustard seeds. Once they crack, add the dried
chilli and hing. Now add minced ginger and chilli. Stir for
a minute and add soaked dal. Further, add the turmeric,
salt, chilli powder and mix well. Add sufficient water to

cook moong dal. Cook covered on low heat. Dal should be separated and not mushy. Lastly, add the lemon juice and garnish with coriander and mix well. Enjoy this side dish with the thali.

Indian Cold Drinks

Rooh Afza

Even today, rooh afza reminds me of rosy nostalgia and takes me back to my childhood. This was a drink that was a must on our summer days. I remember rushing back home in the evening for this cool refreshing drink. Kids will love this drink. You can find rooh afza syrup in many Indian stores.

Ingredients

3.5 cups of chilled water or almond milk

Rooh afza syrup, as per taste

4 tablespoons of basil seeds

Cane sugar, as required (optional)

Ice cubes

How to prepare:

In 3/4 cup of water, soak basil seeds for 30 minutes. To the water, add rooh afza syrup and basil seeds. Now add sugar and roo afza as required. Stir well and enjoy. You can also substitute water with almond milk.

Aam Panna

This summer cooler is a popular drink in India. Unlike many mango beverages, which are made of ripened sweet mangoes, aam panna is made of tender sour mangoes. Mangoes are cooked till soft and mixed with sugar and salt. Blend into a smooth paste and mix with Indian spices.

Ingredients

Pressure cook 1 mango in 2 cups water until soft (5 whistles)

3 tablespoon mint leaves

1/2 teaspoon cumin powder

1/2 teaspoon cardamom powder

1/4 cup unrefined cane sugar

3/4 teaspoon salt

1/2 teaspoon pepper powder

Cold water

A few ice cubes

How to prepare:

Peel the skin off the soft mangoes once cooled. Add the pulp to a blender along with mint and sugar. Blend smooth without water. Now add the rest of the ingredients. Mix well. Now the concentrate is ready. In a tall glass, add a tablespoon of this concentrate, ice cubes, and cold water. Mix well and garnish with mint leaves and enjoy.

Kokum Sharbat

Kokum sharbat is a refreshing cold drink made from kokum fruit concentrate. Kokum fruit is used commonly in Goa and Assamese cuisine in India. This fruit has a sour flavour to it and is hence used as a souring agent in these cuisines. Enjoy this purple drink.

Ingredients

1 1/2 cup dried ripened kokum fruit (soaked in hot water

for 3 hours)

2 cups of cane sugar

2 1/2 cup water

1/4 teaspoon crushed pepper

Pinch of salt

1/2 teaspoon cumin powder

How to prepare:

Blend the kokum into a coarse paste. In a pan, add this paste, 1/2 cup water, and sugar, and let it dissolve completely. Further, boil for 15 minutes, stirring often. Once the mixture gets thick to form a syrup, turn off the heat and add cumin, pepper, and salt. Mix well and sieve the mixture. Squeeze the pulp, and kokum syrup is ready to store in the refrigerator for 2 months. Ina glass with a few ice cubes, add 2 tablespoons of kokum syrup and 2 cups of cold water. Mix well and garnish with mint leaves.

Nimbu Sharbat

Nimbu sharbat is a cold drink that's popular among all parts of India. It's made of fresh lemons. It's not lemonade. It's made of fresh spices and herbs to give it an Indian twist. You will love it.

Ingredients

Lemon juice of 1 lemon

7 ice cubes

1 inch crushed ginger

Pinch of salt

1/4 teaspoon crushed cardamom

5 chopped mint leaves

1 tablespoon cane sugar

1 glass cold water

How to prepare:

In a deep bowl, add all ingredients and mix well. Add ice cubes. Your nimbu sharbat is ready. You can also add rooh afza for a rosy flavour.

Imli Ka Almana

Almana is a tangy summer drink from the deserts of Rajasthan. It is made with tamarind pulp along with spices like cardamom and pepper. Black salt enhances the flavour and mint adds freshness to this drink. Get ready to witness sweet, sour, and tangy flavours at the same time.

Ingredients

2 tablespoon of tamarind

1/2 cup cane sugar

1/2 tablespoon black salt

1/4 teaspoon crushed black pepper powder

1/4 teaspoon cardamom powder

Salt to taste

How to prepare:

Soak tamarind in 1 cup of water. Cover and let it sit for 2 hours.

Now transfer this into a blender and blend to make a smooth paste. Squeeze and strain the pulp with a thin cloth. Add 3 cups of water, pepper, cardamom, salt, black salt. Mix well. Refrigerate for an hour. Pour into 4 glasses and serve chilled.

Panakam

Panakam is a traditional age-old recipe that is offered in temples for a festival called Rama Navami. This is a very common household drink in south India during the summers. It is known to beat the scorching summer heat and cool our body, and it's also known to balance the essential electrolytes in our body.

Ingredients

1/2 cup jaggery

1/4 teaspoon dry ginger powder

2 cups of water or more

Pinch of salt

2 teaspoons black pepper powder

Juice of 1 lemon

1 teaspoon cardamom powder

Pinch of edible camphor (optional)

Cold water

10 tulsi (holy basil leaves) (optional)

How to prepare:

In a bowl, add 2 cups of water and jaggery. mix well and soak for 40 minutes or keep stirring till it dissolves. Now sieve the solution to remove the impurities from jaggery. Now add the jaggery syrup into cold water along with lemon juice, ginger powder, black pepper powder, cardamom powder, and a pinch of salt. Now add a pinch of camphor or skip it. Mix well and serve in glasses and garnish with holy basil leaves.

Chandan Kesar Sherbat

Chandan is sandalwood, and kesar is saffron in Indian terms. Sandalwood is hailed for its cooling properties. This thirst-quenching drink is ideal to beat the heat. This aromatic woody fragrance is to die for.

Ingredients

1 liter of water

3 tablespoons of lemon juice

5 cups of jaggery or cane sugar

2 tablespoons of sandalwood powder

1 teaspoon citric acid (optional)

1 teaspoon crushed saffron

How to prepare:

In a pan, heat half a cup of water and add saffron. Now, turn off the heat and let it sit for 30 minutes. In a pan, add 1 liter of water, lemon juice, and sugar. Boil until the sugar is completely dissolved and sugar syrup is thick. It would take about 5 minutes. Sieve this mixture. Add the sandalwood powder, saffron water, and citric acid to this mixture and combine well. Store this syrup in a glass jar in the refrigerator for a month.

Final Words

I hope you have enjoyed reading my authentic Indian vegan recipes cookbook. Now it's time to wrap it up. However, before doing that, I'd like to thank you for buying my book. NAMASTE!

If there were any teeny tiny mistakes, please excuse me. I've been primarily focused on providing you with the best possible recipes, so I might have erred here and there.

Anyhow, I'd like to take some time and include some vegan cooking tips, which have helped me throughout my journey with veganism. I follow these tips so that I end up cooking healthy and tasty vegan dishes without harming any poor little animals.

Don't shy away from trying out the alternatives. When I say alternatives, I mean the ingredients that can be used in the place of milk, cream, cheese, and any other dairy items. For example, you could use coconut cream, which is derived from a plant. Also, to avoid using animal milk and to still get the taste and flavour of it, try using almond milk. By doing so, you can avoid compromising the taste of your dishes. These plant-based alternatives come with a set of unique and healthy elements, such as vitamins and nutrients.

Do you love mac and cheese? Or do you like to have your popcorn with extra cheese topping? Sadly, vegans can't enjoy that. Well, pretty much everyone loves cheesy food. But, since it's derived from animal by-products, we vegans can't include it in our food. However, there's a very effective and tasty alternative. You can use nutritional yeast in the place of traditional cheese. It tastes the same. Always have nutritional yeast in your kitchen. You know, nutritional yeast is also used in baking your cakes and brewing your beers. So, yeah, it works! Try to maintain adequate stock of this ingredient in your pantry.

Experiment with herbs and spices. I agree that meat tastes scrumptious. And it's hard to re-create such good, tasty meat food with plants. But there's a solution, though. Normally, plant-based dishes taste dull and bland. But that won't be the case if you're smart enough to cook them well.

Adding spices and herbs to your vegan dishes can enhance

the taste by leaps and bounds. In India, we are used to incorporating different types of spices and herbs in our food. In all the recipes I've provided, I made sure that I include some tasty spices and herbs as ingredients.

If you want a better experience, don't shy away from changing the combination of spices. Add your twist, I say!

Oh yeah, we all grew up eating eggs quite often. They taste good, comes with a lot of nutrition, and are also a good energy source. But we vegans care about our cohabitants of this planet, right? We can't take eggs away from the mothers, can we? So, what to do? Well, you can enjoy making egg-based food by replacing animal eggs with eggs made of flax seeds. You can make your eggs by combining flax seed meal of one tablespoon with water of three tablespoons. That's it. You now can cook any dishes with your homemade eggs made of flax seeds.

Keep an eye on your iron and vitamin B12 intake. Iron is a very essential nutrient we need. To be honest, animal meat is a rich resource of this nutrient. Since we don't consume meat, we should find good iron sources.

For that, you should consume leafy greens, legumes, and beans. You can also try including vitamin C rich food, in your diet, as we know that when vitamin C is combined with iron, it's easily absorbable by your body. Coming to vitamin B12, protein sources like tempeh, nutritional yeast, plant milk like soy, almond, coconut, veggies like mushrooms, and humble rice are some rich sources of vitamin B12.

Focus on plant-based proteins. Apart from iron, vegans also miss the luxury of easy protein resources, which are high in animal meat. Don't you worry. There are many ways you can bulk up your protein easily.

Tofu, edamame, tempeh, lentils, beans, and chickpeas are some of the best protein-rich foods. Try consuming oatmeal, quinoa, almonds, and similar plant-based protein-rich foods, so that you don't run out of muscle easily.

I guess it's time to wrap it up, finally! Try to follow these tips as much as you can. Trust me, these have made my life a lot better in leading the vegan lifestyle. We do this because we care for the animals. Moreover, veganism also benefits us a lot by improving our health, both physical and mental.

Again, thanks for reading my book. I wish you a wonderful, healthy, and happy life.

Printed in Great Britain
by Amazon